George Frideric Handel

and Music for Voices

George Frideric Handel

and Music for Voices

Donna Getzinger
Daniel Felsenfeld

620 South Elm Street, Suite 223
Greensboro, North Carolina 27406
http://www.morganreynolds.com

Classical Composers

Johann Sebastian Bach

Antonio Vivaldi

Richard Wagner

Johannes Brahms

George Frideric Handel

GEORGE FRIDERIC HANDEL AND MUSIC FOR VOICES

Library of Congress Cataloging-in-Publication Data

Getzinger, Donna.
  George Frideric Handel and Music for Voices / Donna Getzinger and
Daniel Felsenfeld.
      v. cm. — (Classical composers)
    Includes bibliographical references (p.   ) and index.
    Contents: A Precocious Child — Hamburg — Italian Sojourn — Her Majesty's
Theater — The Music Academy — Handel's Academy — Oratorios —
Competing Troupes — The Messiah — The Last Great Mmasterpieces — Timeline.
      ISBN 1-931798-23-0 (library binding)
      1. Handel, George Frideric, 1685-1759—Juvenile literature. 2.
Composers—Biography—Juvenile literature. [1. Handel, George Frideric,
1685-1759. 2. Composers.] I. Felsenfeld, Daniel. II. Title. III.
Series.
    ML3930.H25G48 2004
    780'.92—dc22

                            2003026729

Printed in the United States of America
First Edition

For Gerrie Getzinger
and in memory of Oleta O'Hara

Contents

Chapter One
A Precocious Child 11

Chapter Two
Hamburg 21

Chapter Three
Italian Sojourn 32

Chapter Four
Her Majesty's Theater 43

Chapter Five
The Royal Academy 60

Chapter Six
Oratorios 77

Chapter Seven
Competing Troupes 90

Chapter Eight
The *Messiah* 100

Chapter Nine
The Last Great Masterpieces 114

Timeline 130
Glossary of Musical Terms 132
Sources 136
Bibliography 139
Web sites 141
Index 142

George Frideric Handel (1685-1759)
(Courtesy of Covent Gardens Archives, Royal Opera House.)

Chapter One
A Precocious Child

When George Frideric Handel was eight years old, his father took him on a trip to the court at Weissenfels, in the German state of Saxony. The elder Handel was a respected physician in the region and served many of the nearby courts. While his father tended to the medical needs of the duke of Weissenfels, Johann Adolf, young George Frideric spent most of his time with his older half-brother, Karl, who was a valet. Karl was supposed to keep an eye on the boy, but somehow George Frideric managed to find his way to the court's chapel, where he encountered an enormous and beautiful pipe organ. Entranced, he approached the instrument and climbed onto the high seat. Although he had never done so before, the child put his hands on the keys and began to play.

A pipe organ is a massive piece of machinery with several

The ornate pipe organ above illustrates the massive size of these impressive instruments. *(Courtesy of Handel House, Halle.)*

keyboards (called manuals) for the hands and the feet, and pipes stretching from floor to ceiling that attach to a wind box the size of a small room. The sound of the music changes according to the amount of air being pushed through the pipes, and the organist controls this airflow by using mechanisms known as stops. Pipe organs of the eighteenth century were played by two people at once: one worked the manuals and stops, and the other pushed giant bellows that blew air into the pipes. No one knows who played the bellows for young George Frideric that day, but the music he made on the giant organ brought the Weissenfels *kapellmeister* (the composer and music director at court) running to the chapel.

The kapellmeister was astonished to find an eight-year-old boy making music on his pipe organ. He immediately reported his discovery to the duke, who, amused by the story of a child sneaking into his chapel, asked to hear George Frideric play. During the next Sunday chapel service, the boy was brought before the duke. His feet barely reached the pedals, and he had never had lessons, but still, he played with confidence. His performance amazed the court. The duke called for George Frideric's father and told him that the boy was a virtuoso whose talent must be trained and nurtured. He ordered George Handel to start his son in music lessons. The duke even suggested young Handel remain in his court where his musical training could be supervised.

George Handel, George Frideric's father, was a distinguished physician who believed in hard work. *(Courtesy of The British Museum, London.)*

Young Handel's father considered music to be a useless career. He wanted his son to attend the university and become a lawyer—a dignified career with a stable and substantial income. The duke's orders put the elder Handel in a difficult spot: he could hardly go against his sovereign's command, no matter how their opinions differed. But he did not want to leave his son in the court and completely abandon him to music.

To obey the duke's wishes without relinquishing his son, Handel performed a neat bit of diplomacy. He asked the duke's permission to hire a music teacher in his hometown of Halle, so, he said, he and his wife could have their son at home. The duke granted his request. George Frideric

Seventeenth-century view of Halle. *(Engraving by Johann Kost and Nikolaus Keyser.)*

could have been a child prodigy and had instant fame in the Weissenfels court, but instead he was taken back to Halle, where George Handel begrudgingly arranged for Wilhelm Zachow, a local organist from the Lutheran church, to teach his son.

As luck would have it, Zachow had tremendous skill at the keyboard. Some of his *cantatas* (short unstaged dramas, usually with religious subject matter, sung by a choir) still exist today. Zachow taught George Frideric everything he knew about playing the organ as well as the oboe, violin, and harpsichord. In addition, he taught the boy to read and write music by having him copy works by master composers from Germany and Italy. His potential as a musician was not consigned to oblivion, as his father wished; George Frideric soaked up every lesson. Meeting Zachow was a fortunate twist of fate in a career, and a life, that would often be guided by forces beyond Handel's control.

Handel was born Georg Friederich Händel on February 23, 1685. Over the course of his life, he would be known as Giorgio Federico Hendel to the people of Italy, Georg Frideric Hændel in France, and George Frideric Handel to the English. His last name would be spelled in a variety of ways.

George Frideric was born to sixty-three-year-old George Handel and his second wife, Dorothea, who was thirty years younger than her husband. Handel's first wife and their oldest child had died during a plague a few years earlier, and Dorothea's first child had died at birth. This made George Frideric the oldest boy of this marriage. Dorothea would give birth to two girls in the coming years.

Young George Frideric bore little resemblance to his father, who was thin and short in stature. He was much more like his thicker and strong-bodied mother. He and his father were nothing alike in personality either. It was the senior Handel's intention to see that his boy would have good schooling and a solid career that would bring pride and respect to the family name. His son, however, saw the world through much more creative, and ambitious, eyes.

We know of Handel's birth from his baptismal record, but there is no record of any detail of his life for the next seven years. Because of this, it is impossible to say exactly when George Frideric began learning to play the harpsichord (a keyboard instrument that predated the piano) but it seems likely his aunt, Anna Taust, may have given him some lessons. The widow of a church pastor, Taust was familiar with church music and could probably play or sing. After the death of her husband, she had come to live with her sister Dorothea's family, so it is very likely that she privately encouraged her musically inclined nephew without his father's permission. The elder Handel would never have approved of such frivolous pursuits.

After the episode at the duke's palace, it was with reluctance that George Handel paid for his son's lessons with Zachow. He held out hope that the boy would realize music was not a suitable career and turn his attentions to law. Despite their differences, father and son were close. When George Handel died in 1697 at age seventy-five, twelve-year-old George Frideric wrote a deeply touching memorial poem for his father, which begins with the verse:

> Ah! bitter grief! my dearest father's heart
>> From me by cruel death is torn away.
> Ah! misery! and ah! the bitter smart
>> Which seizes me, poor orphan from this day.

Handel would always regret that his father did not live to see him become famous, or to hear the beautiful music he would compose.

The surviving Handels were given a pension from the Weissenfels court, but it was only enough to scrape by on. George Frideric's music lessons had to be cancelled. Despite his burgeoning talent, there was just not enough money. Dorothea Handel insisted, as her

Young Handel, as portrayed by Christoph Platz.

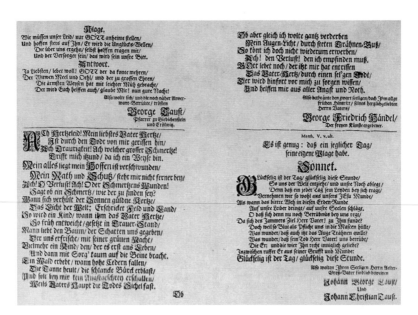

The poem of mourning George Frideric wrote upon his father's death.

husband had, that George Frideric work hard at his studies and earn a solid education. For the rest of his life, Handel worked almost too diligently, seeing little need to socialize or dally in romantic entanglements. His work would occupy all of his thoughts, actions, and time. It was as if he spent the rest of his life proving to the memory of his father that he could succeed, especially because he had rejected the path his father chose for him.

In February of 1702, seventeen-year-old George Frideric Handel enrolled at Halle University. No register remains to prove whether or not Handel took any courses in law, as his father would have wanted. Most likely, he combined law studies with music classes. During that time he met George Phillip Telemann, another law student with musical ambitions, who studied at Leipzig University, only fifty miles

George Phillip Telemann. Considered one of the top composers in eighteenth-century Germany, he is known for his prolific writing in many styles, including operas, cantatas, oratorios, and instrumental works. *(Engraving by Georg Lichtensteger, courtesy of The British Museum.)*

away. Telemann was four years older than Handel and would also become a noted composer. Their friendship spanned decades, and they wrote to each other well into old age.

Only a few months after beginning school, Handel was offered a job as a musician. The local Calvinist church needed a replacement for their organist. The Calvinist doctrine differed some from the Lutheran faith Handel had been raised in. Although both were Protestant religions, the Calvinists had much stricter rules regarding behavior and church ceremonies. In Calvinist services, organists mainly accompanied hymns and played preludes and postludes (music played while parishioners entered or exited the church). The Calvinist church of Halle was willing to overlook Handel's Lutheranism because most of the time their regular organist was too drunk to play services. Any religious qualms Handel had about taking the job were outweighed by the chance to be paid for playing music. Such opportunities were rare in Saxony.

During the 1600s and early 1700s, music, art, architecture, and fashion enjoyed a heyday of interest and innovative design in Italy and France. Today, we call this period the Baroque era. It is characterized by excess in every way—from Louis XIV's luxurious palace at Versailles, with its seven hundred rooms and six thousand paintings, to the elaborately ornamental dress of the wealthy. The architecture favored tall, heavily decorated structures, and Baroque music was filled with rich melodies and musical flourishes.

Technically, the Baroque era reached the fairly conservative German territories of Northern Europe, but the decadent style was tamed somewhat by the area's temperate political and social culture. The recent history of the region we now call Germany contributed to the difference. From 1618-1648 this area had been torn apart by the Thirty Years War, a war fought, at least initially, between Catholic and Protestant rulers. The war eventually became an international conflict, but most of the battles were fought in Germany. There, entire towns were demolished, and marauding armies and troops of scavengers ravaged the land. Those who survived the violence had to rebuild their lives with little food or money, and little assistance from their leaders. It was a dark, miserable time in many ways, and a long way from the extravagance that characterized the Baroque era in Italy and France.

Given the unsettled nature of the economics, politics, and culture of the time, Handel felt lucky to have a job related to music at all. After a year of working at the church in the evenings and on weekends, and attending classes at the university during the day, Handel came to a crossroads in his life. As hard as he tried, school could not capture his attention the way music did. But playing the organ in a Calvinist church was not all that satisfying for him either. He needed to leave his hometown of Halle, to journey to a bigger city where he could meet and study with other musicians. He needed to find a job that involved more than merely playing preludes, postludes, and hymns. Early in 1703, George Frideric Handel said farewell to Halle and journeyed fifty miles north to Hamburg.

Chapter Two
Hamburg

Hamburg, a busy port city along the Elbe River, was different from most cities in the German territories. It had been a free city of the Prussian Empire for almost two hundred years. This meant the city was not ruled by a duke or a prince; instead, the citizens elected *burgermeisters* (mayors), and decided how their tax money would be spent. This walled city had survived the Thirty Years War without much damage to its economy. In 1703 it boasted a population of about 30,000 people making good livings from trade, tourism, and entertainment.

Hamburg had its own opera house and the most famous organist in all of northern Europe, J. Adam Reinken. Though he was eighty years old in 1703, Reinken still played the enormous organ at St. Catherine's Church. Musicians like Handel came from near and far to be part of the exciting musical scene. One of those who came was Johann Sebastian Bach, a young German musician almost exactly Handel's age. The two lived only a few miles apart for several years, but apparently never met. Their careers, and their music, would follow separate paths.

In July, only a few weeks after arriving, Handel met twenty-two year old Johann Mattheson, a musician already established in Hamburg as a composer, singer, and harpsichordist at the Gänsemarkt Opera House. They fast became friends, and spent a great deal of time together that summer taking boating trips, watching the great Reinken perform, and playing practical jokes. Handel was a hard worker, but he also had a wonderful deadpan sense of humor.

In August, the two young men traveled sixty miles north to the town of Lübeck for an audition. Dietrich Buxtehude, the famous organist of St. Marian's Church, was nearing retirement and needed someone to inherit his responsibilities. It was an honorable and high-profile position, but Handel and Mattheson appeared to have trouble taking the audition process seriously. "We played on almost all the organs and harpsichords in the place," wrote Mattheson, "and made an agreement that . . . he should only play the organ and I only the harpsichord."

Perhaps neither of the young men was really interested in the position, for, as Mattheson went on to record, there was a catch: "It turned out that there was some marriage condition proposed in connection with the appointment, for which neither of us felt the slightest inclination, so we said goodbye to the place, after having enjoyed ourselves ex-

The famous organist J. Adam Reinken at the keyboard. Pictured with him are Johann Thiele (playing cello) and Dietrich Buxtehude, also major figures in seventeenth-century German music. *(Courtesy of Museum für Hamburgische Geschichte.)*

tremely, and received many gratifying tributes of respect." It was not unusual for marriage to be part of a job offer but, apparently, the offer of Buxtehude's daughter as a bride had little appeal to either Handel or Mattheson.

The two returned to Hamburg in high spirits. Mattheson helped his friend find a job teaching music to the British ambassador's son, a position that gave Handel a chance to learn about London. He was fascinated by stories of the city's huge buildings, grand houses, elaborate parks, theaters, opera houses, and circuses. Every detail excited Handel, and he began to dream about someday making the long journey to see London for himself.

When Hamburg's theater season began (a theater season is the series of months, usually October through June, when

Johann Mattheson, one of the first friends Handel made in Hamburg. *(The British Museum, London.)*

operas and plays are staged), Mattheson found Handel a position playing violin in the Gänsemarkt Opera orchestra. Orchestras of the time were much smaller than they are today. Soon the conductor realized that, although Handel was a passable violinist, he excelled at the harpsichord, and he was promoted into that position.

Handel's early experiences with opera were good for him. Both he and Mattheson considered themselves to be budding composers. Mattheson's work was more sophisticated and urbane, while Handel's repertoire consisted mainly of church pieces. As much as Mattheson liked Handel and appreciated his talent at the keyboard, he knew his friend needed exposure to other kinds of music. "At that time," Mattheson wrote, "he composed very long, long airs, and really interminable cantatas which had neither the right kind of skill nor of taste, though complete in harmony, but the lofty schooling of opera soon trimmed him into other fashions."

In the Baroque era, opera was considered the highest

form of musical entertainment. It had only come into existence one hundred years earlier, when the first opera, *Orfeo,* by Claudio Monteverdi, premiered in Italy in 1607. Over time, the form had evolved, expanding in length and including comic and serious elements, dance and theater. The opera house was the center of activity in any city—a place of constant spectacle. Rich and poor alike came, sometimes several times a week, to see the shimmering sets and gorgeous costumes, and to hear the newest arias (vocal solos). They came to hear the famous singers, some of

Claudio Monteverdi (1567-1643) is credited with being the father of modern opera. His *Orfeo,* which premiered in 1607, incorporated elements of theater, music, and dance. *(Courtesy of Tiroler Museum Ferdinandeum, Innsbruck.)*

whom rose to prominence and received generous salaries. Because the country still felt the effects of the Thirty Years War, German opera houses were not as successful as their Italian counterparts, but they still paid top fees to attract the best singers.

Even though the music was exciting, the main reason people attended the opera was to socialize. Theaters were built in such a fashion that the rich sat in boxes that faced each other rather than the stage. Those who could not afford box seats stood on the main floor (the gallery). The orchestra was in plain sight, often on the stage itself, and the theaters were fully lit during the entire performance. It was not uncommon for the audience to talk and laugh throughout the show, pausing only to listen to a favorite aria or to applaud a celebrated singer's appearance.

Musicians, actors, and theater directors had to work tremendously hard, with dozens of operas to memorize and multiple performances in any given week. A dramatic German tragedy might play one night and two nights later an Italian comedy would hit the stage. Audiences did not listen to the operas very closely, but, even so, would only sit through the same show once or twice. New operas had to be written, and were, at break-neck speed, in order to keep patrons buying tickets.

The director of the Gänsemarkt Opera House in Hamburg was a German composer named Richard Keiser. He was prolific, with more than one hundred twenty works to his name. In the twilight of his career by the time Handel appeared, Keiser had decided to enjoy his fame and wealth

A scene from a Baroque opera production. *(Courtesy of Robert Halding Picture Library.)*

and was no longer very dedicated to his duties as a composer. Often he was too drunk to lead the performances, in which case Mattheson or Handel would do the job, since operas were generally conducted from the harpsichord.

Keiser was impressed by Handel's talent and gradually began to give more responsibility to the young man. The two collaborated on an important piece and while Keiser got the credit for it, word spread that Handel had done most of the work. Handel met a writer named Friedrich Christian Feustking, who had written a libretto (script) for a new opera called *Almira.* Keiser was supposed to write the music for the upcoming season, but he was unable to do the work. Handel offered to write it instead.

It is not fully clear how Mattheson felt about Handel

George Frideric Handel at the keyboard. *(Painting by Sir James Thornhill.)*

taking on this new, promising responsibility. But their friendship began to suffer around this time as they began competing with each other. The tension reached a boiling point during a performance of *Cleopatra,* an opera composed by and starring Mattheson. After he performed the death scene of his character Antonius, Mattheson would come back on stage and direct the remainder of the opera from his place at the harpsichord. During one performance, in December 1704, Handel was filling in at the harpsichord and refused to give up his seat.

They managed to get through the rest of the performance, but as soon as the opera concluded, the two musicians stepped outside and drew their swords. Handel would likely have died that night, had not Mattheson's blade shattered when it hit a brass button on his coat. Their friendship was repaired, as Mattheson writes: "No harm came of the affair, and through the intervention of one of the most eminent counselors in Hamburg, as well as of the manager of the Opera House, we were soon reconciled again; and I had the honour, on the same day, 30 December, of entertaining Handel to dinner after which we went in the evening to the rehearsal of *Almira,* and became better friends than before."

Despite what Mattheson wrote, the friendship would never be quite the same; it had been soured by professional rivalry. Mattheson would later star in one of Handel's operas, but the two young men would never be the "better friends" that Mattheson claimed. They stayed in contact all of their lives, but Handel's letters to Mattheson focus mostly on business. Handel corresponded with Telemann and others, too, but he learned from this experience that, for him, business and pleasure should not mix. He would never again have such a close friendship with a professional associate.

On January 8, 1705, *Almira* opened at the Gänsemarkt Opera House. The opera takes place in a Spanish court and is a huge affair full of pomp, costume parades, and dances. Most operas were written in Italian because it was considered a more sophisticated language. Operas written in German were regarded as inferior, but they were also the only pieces most German people could understand. So, *Almira* was written half in German and half in Italian. The story may have been confusing and hard to follow, but it was a huge success in spite of this. There was such demand that the opera was repeated twenty times in a three-week period.

Buoyed by this success, Handel quickly followed with another opera, composed in less than a month. This piece

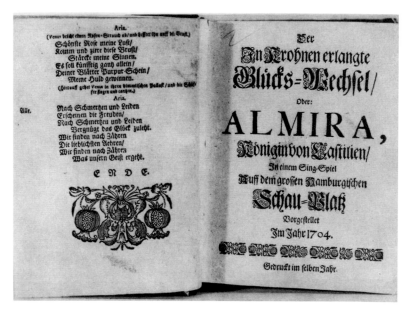

Handel composed the music for *Almira* in 1704, the year this printed edition was released. The opera was first performed in 1705.

was called *Die durch Blut und Mord erlangte Liebe, oder: Nero (Love Obtained by Blood and Murder, or: Nero)*. No score of this opera survives, but Nero, the tyrannical Roman emperor, must have made for a fascinating subject. The opera did not repeat the success enjoyed by *Almira*. After only three performances, the theaters closed down for Lent (the weeks between Ash Wednesday and Easter, during which Christians gave up worldly pleasures). By the time Lent was over, the opera company was struggling financially and could not afford to restage *Nero*.

Handel did not write an opera for the 1705-6 season, nor are there records indicating he played in the orchestra. It seems he took time off to dedicate himself to composing. He had made a good amount of money from *Almira*—

enough to buy him some time away from the hectic world of the theater. Already a financially shrewd entrepreneur, he knew that another big hit would be worth much more than the money he could earn playing in the orchestra.

One piece he wrote during this time was an epic opera called *Florindo und Daphne,* which has also been lost to time. A love story with more than one hundred musical numbers, the opera was so long that it had to be split into two performances of three acts each. The 1706-1707 opera season was chaotic, so *Florindo und Daphne* was not scheduled until January 1708. It was performed only once, and Handel was not there to see it. By that time, he had left Hamburg for Italy.

While in Hamburg, Handel had met a number of influential people from all over Europe. One of his more important and generous patrons was Prince Gian Gastone de' Medici, son of the Prince of Tuscany. Gian Gastone was a minor figure in the powerful Medici family, but he was wealthy and loved music and art. He encouraged Handel to come to Florence with him, promising to cover all expenses. Although the greatest days of the Italian Renaissance were over, Italy remained the center of music and art. Handel knew he would improve his prospects by spending time there. He accepted the prince's offer and left Hamburg in the autumn of 1706.

Chapter Three
Italian Sojourn

Twenty-one-year-old Handel could hardly have been prepared for what he found in Florence, Italy. He left the cold, dreary climate of Germany for the sunny and warm Mediterranean, and found ornate palaces and cathedrals there that made the functional buildings of Hamburg seem even plainer. Extravagantly ornamental Catholicism in Italy replaced Germany's more austere Protestantism. While vastly different culturally, the two countries were similar in one respect: they were both made up of a hodgepodge of independent city-states and republics, each with its own government. No king or emperor reigned over the territories as a whole. In Italy, though, rulers governed primarily according to the wishes of the Catholic pope.

Handel stayed in Florence only a few months, until January 1707. He was enthralled by the beautiful countryside, the friendly people, and, above all, the reverence Italians had for music. While in Florence, Handel dedicated his composing efforts mainly to cantatas. About one hundred of these cantatas still survive. The people of Italy gave Handel the nickname *Il Sassone* (the Saxon, after his home region) as a sign of their approval.

From Florence, Handel traveled to Rome, Italy's capital city. The Medici princes had given him letters of introduction to influential church leaders, which eased his transition. He gave an organ performance in the San Giovanni church on January 14, 1707, where he played "to the amazement of everybody." Handel had no problem finding wealthy patrons to support him. The most significant of these was Cardinal Ottoboni.

Ottoboni was the most powerful man in Rome besides the pope. He had the money and the power to support artists he liked. The composer and harpsichordist Domenico Scarlatti and the violinist Arcangelo Corelli both worked for Ottoboni. Scarlatti, the son of composer Alessandro Scarlatti, was highly regarded for his writing and his playing. Corelli was quickly becoming known as the master of the concerto (a form of instrumental music that Corelli helped to establish, in which a soloist plays with an orchestra). Handel's being invited into this company was truly an honor.

As far as opera was concerned, though, Rome was not the best place for Handel, mainly because the pope had forbidden opera throughout the city. There was still a thirst for dramatic music, and composers satisfied it by writing works that were similar in length, structure, and musical

Francesco Trevisani's portrait of Cardinal Ottoboni. *(Courtesy of The Bowes Museum.)*

style to operas, but in which the singers did not "act." Called oratorios, they differed from opera because they were not staged and had no costumes or scenery. They were nearly always about religious subjects, whereas operas generally had secular (non-religious) plots.

The first oratorio Handel wrote for Rome was called *Il Trionfo del Tempo e del Disinganno (The Triumph of Time and Truth)* and it premiered in May 1707. The libretto was written by another man of the cloth, Cardinal Pamphili. The plot, which had characters representing Truth and Time being tempted by Beauty and Pleasure, was not terribly interesting. The power of the piece came from its music. In Rome, Handel was writing for the top musicians in all of Europe. He wrote dazzling arias and solos for instruments including the oboe, organ, cello, and violin. Some of the music was so complicated that even Corelli

Arcangelo Corelli (1653-1713).

had difficulty playing it, and he was considered the best violinist in Italy.

After the success of his first oratorio, both Cardinal Ottoboni and Cardinal Pamphili offered Handel rooms in their palaces. Although he was honored, he wanted to find a patron who was not so closely tied to the Catholic Church. Savvy as ever, Handel knew he would be under fewer constraints if not associated with such a powerful organization.

A better offer came from an Italian prince, Marchese Francesco Ruspoli. He offered Handel a room in his palace, meals at the royal table, and all the luxuries afforded the ruling class, in exchange for composing cantatas and other small pieces for regular weekly performances. Handel made it clear to Ruspoli that there was no binding commitment between them, that he needed to be free to compose for

Alessandro Scarlatti. *(Courtesy of Civico Museo Bibliografico Musicale, Bologna.)*

whomever he chose and to travel whenever he liked. The idea of being forced into one job, working under only one patron, was too much of a threat to his creativity. Handel always fought to stay free of arrangements that would make him obligated to any one person, which was unusual behavior for a musician of his time.

Ruspoli turned out to be an ideal patron. He acquiesced to Handel's request for the freedom to travel, and Handel was often on the move. Two trips were particularly significant: the first time he left Ruspoli's palace and the last.

In the fall of 1707, Handel left Rome to return to Florence. Amazingly, in between the oratorios, cantatas, and smaller works, he had also managed to complete his first full Italian opera, *Rodrigo,* which was to be performed at the city theater, *Teatro Civico Accademico,* in November. Many historians believe that Handel actually composed some of the music for *Rodrigo* back in his Hamburg days. He may also have borrowed some music from his earlier opera, *Almira,* for *Rodrigo's* overture (opening music). Handel was a quick composer, but even he would have had to work without sleep to produce so much material in only half a year's time.

Many composers incorporated recycled portions of earlier works into their new pieces—the practice is called parody. Since most operas only had one run on the stage, it was unlikely anyone would recognize a tune if it was lifted and shifted from one piece to another.

Handel, though, differed from his contemporaries in his willingness to appropriate large chunks of works that were not his own—a practice we now call plagiarism. No one knows for certain how Handel was able to get away with calling music written by other musicians his own. Of course he was always under pressure to produce new works, but that hardly excuses stealing. Whatever the motive and the means, Handel would appropriate from the works of others over the course of his career.

There is some reason to suspect that Handel had his one and only love affair during this stay in Florence. Victoria Tarquini was a talented singer and a favorite of Prince Ferdinand. She starred in an opera being performed in Florence at the same time as *Rodrigo,* and the rumors about her affair with Handel show up in the personal letters of Electress Sophia of Hanover. She wrote that Handel "is a good looking man and talk is that he was the lover of Victoria." Nothing came of the relationship, though. Perhaps Handel was more discreet in subsequent relationships, or perhaps he rejected romance altogether in order to dedicate himself to his art—either way, the composer was never again publicly linked with a lover, and he never married.

In 1709, two years after his first trip, Handel left Ruspoli's patronage, and Rome, for the last time. He headed north to the beautiful city of canals, Venice. Cardinal Vincenzo Grimani, whose family owned the San Giovanni Grisostomo Theater, had written a libretto for an opera titled *Agrippina,* which is a comedy loosely based on a bit of ancient Roman history about a highly immoral empress. He wanted Handel to compose the music in time for Carnival season. (Carnival is the celebratory period that takes place in Catholic countries before Lent begins.)

Venice was the opposite of Rome in many ways. It had

Venice, Italy's lagoon city. Below, typical Venetian boats, called gondolas, crowd the canals. *(Courtesy of The Academia, Venice.)*

The San Giovanni Grisostomo Theater in Venice. *(Courtesy of Musei Veneziani d'Arte e di Storia, Venice.)*

been the center of its own empire for over eight hundred years. It had its own government, and the power of the Catholic Church was felt less here than anywhere else in Italy. Venice's strong economy depended on its key position along the trade routes between Europe and Asia. The lagoon city was also a popular destination because of its beauty and its incredible music. Operas and concerts were performed in the many grand theaters, gondoliers sang as they ferried their boats along the canals, fruit sellers played instruments on the cobbled streets, and Sunday Masses were elaborate, dramatic spectacles. Every year between Christmas and Lent, Venice erupted into Carnival season, a time of gaiety, festivities, and lavish performances. Each theater strove to put on the best new shows with the brightest stars, and people came from all over the world to see them.

Handel had visited Venice briefly once before, with Domenico Scarlatti during the Carnival season of 1708. He met Cardinal Grimani then and soon realized that he needed to be in that city if he wanted to make something of his opera writing. When Grimani sent him the libretto to *Agrippina,* Handel jumped at the chance to return there and to have his music performed by some of the finest musicians in Italy. (One of those musicians was Antonio Vivaldi, a Venetian who would go on to compose numerous works himself, most notably *The Four Seasons.*)

The opening nights of *Agrippina* were so successful that the opera ran for an unprecedented twenty-seven performances. Legend has it that Duke Ernst August of Hanover attended every show. The duke was enthralled with Handel's music and suggested to the twenty-four-year-old composer that he relocate to Hanover. Handel had received job offers from various courts in Germany, but working in Hanover seemed most promising because the best theaters were there. Handel's time in Italy had impacted his music tremendously. He became a more sophisticated and urbane composer, and in March of 1710, he took his new knowledge back to his native land.

Handel went home to Halle to visit his family for a couple of months before moving on to Hanover. There he learned that his older sister had recently married and that the younger one had died. He gave to his mother and surviving sister a silver plate he had received from Prince Ferdinand de' Medici in honor of his composition *Rodrigo.* Before long he was back on the road again.

Elector George Lud-
wig governed the city of
Hanover, which was
north of the Saxon terri-
tory where Handel was
born. Through a com-
plicated lineage, the
Hanover elector was ex-
pected to become king
of England when the cur-
rent monarch, Queen
Anne, died. She had a
nephew who was the
king of Scotland, but ev-
eryone expected her to
pass the throne to George
Ludwig. When Handel

George Ludwig, Elector of Hanover, the future King George I, was a great supporter of Handel's music. *(Courtesy of National Portrait Gallery, London.)*

came to the court, in 1710, the news was that Queen Anne's
health had been steadily deteriorating. The elector and his
ministers were far too busy preparing themselves to rule two
kingdoms to pay much attention to the music written for
court events.

Some composers might have balked at such a situation,
but it was perfect for Handel. Characteristically, he did not
want to feel tied down to any one post or obligated to any
royal leader. He wanted to continue composing operas that
would have commercial success. He also wanted to keep
traveling. Duke Ernst August wanted Handel to remain at
his post in Hanover so badly that he offered to grant the

young composer as much as a twelve-month leave of absence whenever he liked. In addition, his salary would be extremely high. He earned about twenty times as much as Johann Sebastian Bach, who held the same position of kapellmeister at another court.

The possibility of their ruler soon becoming king of England meant that everyone in Hanover talked constantly about that distant land. Within a few short weeks, Handel's old curiosity about England had been rekindled. Upon receiving an invitation to the court of Düsseldorf, a German city about halfway between Hanover and England, to play and write some music, Handel requested his first long-term leave of absence. Once his obligations in Düsseldorf were complete, Handel continued westward—all the way to London.

Chapter Four
Her Majesty's Theater

Handel's journey to London was not easy. He traveled by carriage across Germany to the coast, then on a boat across the channel. Trains were more than a century away, and land travel meant slow, bumpy, dirty rides, even in the finest of coaches. When he finally arrived in London, he was bitterly disappointed.

Compared to the bright, wealthy cities of Italy and the luxurious courts of Germany, London was gray and dull, foggy and cold. Although the upper classes spent fortunes building lavish houses and parks for strolling, the majority of the city had been built hastily along the narrow, winding streets. These streets were full of filth and a shocking amount of noise. The majority of the population consisted of poor workers or shopkeepers with little time for art and music; the most popular amusements were wrestling and

Old London Bridge, 1746

cock fighting (a sport where spectators bet on which of two roosters would defeat the other). The streets seemed to be full of beggars, pickpockets, and thugs.

Some theater impresarios (producers) of London had been trying to convince theatergoers for more than a decade that opera, and especially Italian opera, was worth spending money on, but Londoners preferred plays. The great English playwright William Shakespeare had been dead for a century but his legacy lived on in the enduring popularity of his plays. Opera plots were considered weak and inferior—and Italian operas were not even comprehensible.

Still, producers at the various theaters around the city forged ahead, determined to win audiences over to opera. They started bit by bit by adding music to the plays. In 1700 and again in 1704, a half-sung, half-spoken play called *Dido and Aeneus* won some acclaim as the first "musical." Two years later the first successful opera, an English adaptation of *Camilla* by the Italian composer Giovanni Bononcini won the respect of audiences. Two years after that, Alessandro Scarlatti's *Pirro e Demitrio* was performed in London, half in English and half in Italian.

Only one year before Handel arrived, in 1710, did London witness two successful full-length Italian works. It was not, however, the music or the stories that drew the crowds. The producers finally figured out that the key to the success of Italian opera was importing famous singers and composers from Italy. Audiences would show up to see and hear these international superstars. However, a full season made up only of opera had yet to play in London, and without a core group of able composers, librettists, and singers it never would.

Handel's name was familiar to some Londoners even before his arrival there. Those from the upper classes who had toured continental Europe might have encountered his music abroad, and some of it had already been brought to London to be used as background music for plays. English acquaintances he had made in Italy and Germany knew of his impending visit and talked up his talent. Also, as everyone in London was interested in the doings of the future king of England, they had great interest in a young man recently arrived from the Hanover court.

Word spread quickly, and within a few days of his arrival, Handel was approached by Aaron Hill, a wealthy businessman who managed an opera house in the aristocratic business center of London known as the Haymarket. Built in

1705, this opulent theater was called the Queen's Theater, or Her Majesty's Theater, because it was supported by Queen Anne and performances there were put on largely to please her. If she wanted to see a certain production, it would be staged on the night she wanted to attend. Hill must have been thrilled at the prospect of hosting a Handel production—all of London would want tickets to see the next monarch's court composer.

Hill asked Handel to compose an opera to the libretto of *Rinaldo,* written by Giacomo Rossi. Handel accepted—this was exactly what he had come to London to do. He amazed everyone with how quickly he composed. "Mr. Handel," wrote Rossi, "the Orpheus of our century, while composing the music, scarcely gave me time to write, and to my great wonder I saw an entire opera put to music by that surprising genius, with the greatest degree of perfection, in only two weeks." Rossi didn't know that Handel cheated a bit by using parts of some of his earlier music.

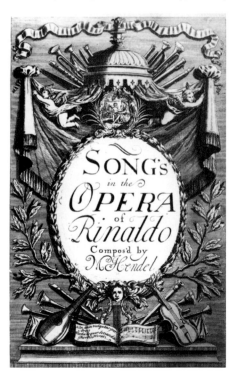

Title page for the published songs of Handel's *Rinaldo. (Courtesy of The British Library, London.)*

On the night after Handel's twenty-sixth birthday, February 24, 1711, London witnessed the opening of *Rinaldo*. It went over tremendously well, earning fifteen repeat performances through the end of June. In April, halfway through the season, a publisher named John Walsh bought the rights to publish the score. He made a fortune in sales, seventy times what he had paid the composer, and Handel joked that next time they should switch roles: Walsh would write the music and Handel would publish it. The two went on to have long, prosperous careers together.

It was not only his opera that won Handel fame and recognition; Queen Anne expressed her support as well, as the newspapers declared with this announcement: "Tuesday, the 6th of February, being the Queen's Birth-day . . . was perform'd a fine Consort being a Dialogue in Italian, in Her Majesty's Praise, set to excellent Musick by the famous Mr. Hendel . . . with which Her Majesty was extremely well pleas'd."

There is no record that the Queen ever attended Handel's operas. Her health was precarious, and she did not often leave the palace. However, her blessing of Handel's music was noted by every member of London's upper class. Handel's name would not soon be forgotten.

With June came the anniversary of Handel's first year of employment in Hanover—and he had hardly been there for any of it. He had to leave London in order to fulfill his obligations to the court. For the next year-and-a-half Handel stayed faithful to Hanover, composing mainly small vocal pieces. In particular, he put together a set of twelve Italian

Queen Anne, in an engraving by E. C. Heiss.

duets for Princess Caroline (although only five of them were original, the other seven had been copied from other works).

In London, his opera *Rinaldo* continued to be performed at Her Majesty's Theater. Handel was eager to return to the city and further his success. In the summer of 1712, he received another libretto from Rossi titled *Il Pastor Fido (The Faithful Shepherd)*. The story involves Diana, the Roman goddess of the hunt, who tries to persuade a hunter, Silvio, to marry Amarilli, a shepherdess. Handel set it to music and requested a second leave of absence from Hanover to take his new opera to London for an October premiere. The Elector of Hanover gave Handel permission to go for one full year. Once Handel stepped onto English soil, though, he had no intention of ever leaving.

While Handel was gone, the popularity of Italian opera in London had again declined. Except for nine productions of *Rinaldo,* there had been no profitable opera stagings. Meanwhile, Aaron Hill and several of the librettists and composers left Her Majesty's Theater to work elsewhere and the Italian singing stars left England altogether. The new manager, Owen MacSwiney, was not nearly as business-minded as Hill had been, but he was smart enough to stage Handel's new opera when the composer showed up in October 1712.

Il Pastor Fido, which opened on November 26, 1712, did not fare nearly as well as *Rinaldo.* Handel had tried to adopt a less flamboyant composing style—perhaps attempting to make the opera seem less typically Italian to the English audience. Alas, he was wrong. Those Londoners who enjoyed Italian opera loved it precisely for its excesses. One contemporary wrote of his disappointment in the *Opera Register,* a newspaper about the London theater scene: "The Scene represented only the Country of Arcadia, ye [the] Habits [costumes] were old, ye Opera Short." *Il Pastor Fido* had only six performances.

Handel was quick to recognize what his audiences wanted, and he sought new librettos that would have more appeal. He began working with Nicola Francesco Haym on the first of several collaborations. Together they created *Teseo (Theseus).* In this work the Greek hero Theseus disguises himself to defend his father and win the crown. A vicious love triangle results when both father and son fall in love with the same woman, Agilea. Handel finished the five-act score within a month's time. It was ready for a premiere performance on January 10, 1713.

The London theater crowd rushed to this new opera: the first two nights of *Teseo* were completely sold out. After the second performance, MacSwiney, fearing that the good fortune would not last, stole all the box office earnings and fled England. This swindle could have been a major problem for Handel, because neither the scenery nor the singers' salaries had been paid. However, a Swiss count and astute businessman, Johann Jacob Heidegger, stepped up to help. Heidegger took over the management of Her Majesty's Theater for the remainder of the season, and it was able to show a small profit when it broke for the summer.

In 1713, Richard Boyle was a wealthy nineteen-year-old patron of the arts with a great interest in architecture. Having a great mind himself, he made a hobby of surrounding himself with geniuses. One politician of the era remembered, "He [Boyle] possessed every quality of a genius and artist except envy." Wisely, Handel had dedicated *Teseo* to Boyle, who was immediately captivated by the composer. Handel agreed to write music for Boyle's social engagements in return for rooms in Burlington House (Boyle's massive estate in the heart of the city) and all the privi-

Johann Jacob Heidegger was a key figure in the London theater world for four decades. *(Engraving by John Faber.)*

leges of the noble class. Handel hobnobbed with members of both the London aristocracy and the art world, and with every social engagement he increased his reputation and widened his circle of influence.

Though Handel was a famous composer and visible social figure, he was very reserved about his private affairs. No personal letters or diaries survive to give insight into who were his closest

Richard Boyle, third Earl of Burlington (1694-1753). His support of select English architects, and his own architectural designs, established the accepted style in England during the eighteenth century. *(Courtesy of the National Portrait Gallery, London.)*

friends, or what he was like in the company of so many distinguished people. We do know that he had a healthy appetite and grew quite stout thanks to the heaping plates of food he was served at Burlington House. Handel was also often seen drinking a glass of ale and chatting with friends at local taverns. On these occasions, his companions usually cajoled him into playing the harpsichord so they could sing and dance. Handel must have been, at this point in his life,

Burlington House *(Engraving by Johannes Kip, courtesy of Guildhall Library.)*

a pleasant, amicable man, or he would not have stayed long in favor with the members of Boyle's social circle.

Queen Anne turned forty-eight years old on February 6, 1713. Even though she had her own court composer, Handel took it upon himself to write a birthday ode for her. Called *Eternal Source of Light Divine,* the piece took as its refrain the words "The day that gave great Anna birth, who fix'd a lasting peace on earth." The music impressed the ailing queen so much that she commissioned Handel to write something to celebrate the upcoming Peace of Utrecht.

England, allied with Holland and the Hapsburg (Austrian) Empire, had been fighting to strip France and Spain of power outside their borders. The war was eventually brought to an end by a series of treaties between the warring countries. England and the Hapsburg Empire emerged victorious as France and Spain were forced to cede some of their territory. Elector George Ludwig in Hanover was furious about the settlements, for he knew they would only cause problems when the defeated countries regained their strength. He held his tongue, though, fearing that Queen Anne would give her throne to her nephew in Scotland.

A cartoon of Handel with a pig's snout, playing the organ while surrounded by heaps of food. He gained a reputation for his large appetite. *(Courtesy of the Gerald Coke Handel Collection.)*

Handel was not a political man. He ignored the implications the treaties had for his current employer, the future king, focusing instead on honoring the queen who had made them possible. He wrote *Utrecht Te Deum* and *Jubilate* for presentation at the Chapel Royal on July 5, 1714, but the sickly queen was too weak to attend the performance. A few weeks later, Handel played them for her in a private concert. She was so impressed that she arranged an annual pension of two hundred pounds per year for the rest of his life—a substantial sum in those days.

By July, the opera season in London was long over and Handel should have returned to Hanover months before. But the combination of his comfortable lodgings at Burlington House and having the queen's approval made Handel want to stay in London and prepare for the next season. When Elector George Ludwig heard that Handel intended to stay in England and had been given a pension by the royal court, he fired the composer. This must have given Handel a fright, for the elector would be coming to England soon enough as heir to the throne, and being out of favor with the king could damage his career. Fortunately for Handel, a month after his firing Handel was brought back into the service of the elector of Hanover. Between his Hanover salary and his yearly pension from the queen of England, twenty-eight-year-old Handel was now the richest composer in the world.

Less than a month later, on August 1, 1714, Queen Anne died. She was forty-nine years old. It took a few months for King George I to conclude his activities in Hanover and take over his duties in England. His coronation took place on October 20, 1714 and one of his first public appearances in England was a church service where a piece by Handel was performed. King George I renewed his fondness for Handel's work, even becoming a fan of his operas.

The king's pleasure in Handel's music was confirmed in 1715 when he invited the famous violinist Francesco Geminiani to play at the palace. Geminiani brought Handel along to accompany him on the harpsichord. King George I was so pleased with the performance that he ordered Handel's annual stipend from Queen Anne doubled. At the same time, the Princess of Wales (the king's daughter-in-law) hired Handel to teach music to her two daughters and offered him a substantial salary for this work. Both of the girls were quite skilled on the harpsichord, so the job must have been more a pleasure than a burden for the famous composer.

That same year, Handel had his first big opera success since *Teseo* two years earlier. Johann Jacob Heidegger was still running operations at the theater in the Haymarket (now called *His* Majesty's Theater) and had given Handel a libretto by Nicola Haym called *Amadigi,* about a love triangle compounded by sorcery. This opera premiered on May 25, 1715. The arias in this work were so popular that audiences requested to hear them repeated over and over during the performances. Although this was quite flattering to Handel and the stars, it made the opera intolerably long— sometimes lasting more than five hours. A notice had to be issued by the theater management: "Whereas by the frequent calling for the songs again, the operas have been too tedious; therefore the singers are forbidden to sing any song above once; and it is hope nobody will call for 'em, or take it ill when not obeyed."

The following summer Handel took a trip to Germany in the entourage of King George I. He had a chance then to visit his mother and sister, and while at home he took into his service an old colleague named John Christopher Smith. Smith returned to London with Handel and worked as a music copyist and personal assistant. A few years later, Smith's son (John Christopher Smith, Junior) would also come to London to be in Handel's personal employ. Handel had a very close partnership with both father and son for the rest of his life. He must have been a pleasant and generous employer to lure the Smiths away from their homeland and to keep them contented for the next four decades.

It was also during this trip to Germany that Handel composed a Passion (a sacred work about the life and death of Jesus Christ). His music accompanied a poem by Barthold Heinrich Brockes called *Der für die Sünde der Welt gemarterte und sterbende Jesus* (otherwise known as *Brockes Passion*). It was well received in Germany; Telemann directed it several times in Leipzig, and Bach, now

kapellmeister at the court of Cöthen, copied it and studied it diligently. Many believe the operatic structure of *Brockes Passion* inspired the two Passion masterpieces Bach wrote later in his own career. Handel, however, now considered himself an Englishman who wrote Italian operas, and never wrote a German work again.

Duke Johann Adolf VI influenced the decision to mount the festivities on the Thames that included Handel's *Water Music*. He first met Handel in Venice, in 1709. *(Portrait by Michael Dahl.)*

When the king and his party returned to England, they found that the English public had grown hostile toward the new ruler. The London aristocrats did not like the way George I flaunted his mistresses, nor were they pleased that, so far, he had refused to speak a word of English. They thought he was too loyal to Hanover and was going to neglect England in favor of his homeland. To smooth ruffled feathers, the

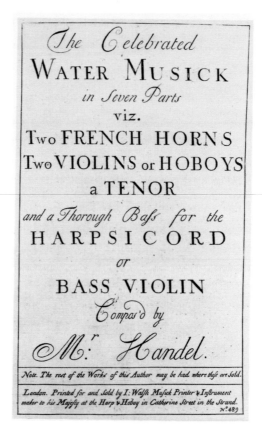

The Celebrated
WATER MUSICK
in Seven Parts
viz.
Two FRENCH HORNS
Two VIOLINS or HOBOYS
a TENOR
and a Thorough Bass for the
HARPSICORD
or
BASS VIOLIN
Compos'd by
Mr Handel.

Note. The rest of the Works of this Author may be had where these are Sold.

London. Printed for and Sold by I: Walsh Musick Printer & Instrument maker to his Majesty at the Harp & Hoboy in Catherine Street in the Strand.
Nº 489

Title page of the first edition of Handel's *Water Music. (Courtesy of the Gerald Coke Handel Collection.)*

king arranged a spectacle—a magnificent celebration to take place in boats on the Thames. He asked Handel to write the music for this special occasion, which happened on July 17, 1717.

The grand orchestral piece Handel wrote for the boat party turned out to be one of his most famous and enduring instrumental works. Entitled *Water Music,* it was played by fifty musicians on a barge floating alongside the king's boat. One eyewitness wrote, "His majesty approved of it so greatly that he caused it to be repeated three times in all, although each performance lasted an hour—namely twice before and once after supper." The work remains extremely popular today.

The king helped Handel to build his reputation in London, but simultaneously, and unintentionally, he made Handel's operatic career more difficult. In this era an opera house had to be patronized by the noble class in order to succeed. If the king and his court gave their nod of approval, ticket sales surged; if they ignored or disliked an opera, sales would plummet. In 1717, box-office numbers were at an all-time low. This was not because the king disliked opera, but was the result of a feud with his oldest son, the Prince of Wales.

King George I and the Prince of Wales had started their fight at the christening of the prince's son, Prince George William, in November 1717. The prince was angry that his father restricted his power and his ability to speak directly to Parliament. As the bad feelings grew, the king declared that the prince and his family were no longer allowed to enter St. James Palace. Then the king and the prince refused to be in the same place at the same time. This affected the opera at His Majesty's Theater, because if the king and prince did not appear, others stayed away as well. Salaries could not be covered; scenery and costumes could not be paid for. Heidegger finally closed the doors that winter, unsure if the theater would ever reopen.

Handel was in a difficult position. He received his pension from the king, but was also paid by the prince for tutoring his daughters. It would be unwise to favor one royal family member over the other, so he could not work exclusively for either court. A solution presented itself at the end of 1717. The earl of Carnarvon (soon to be the duke of Chandos) had built a magnificent palace, called Cannons, just outside of London. He offered Handel a job as composer-in-residence. He would be given free room and board and would be paid handsomely for very little effort. Eager to be out of the public eye until the royal feud died down, Handel accepted the job. It would be three years before he would write another opera for the public, and then he would do so on his own terms.

Chapter Five
The Royal Academy

From 1717 through most of 1719 Handel lived a quiet life at Cannons. He composed anthems (hymns of praise or loyalty) for the chapel, as well as ceremonial pieces for important events. Among the important works that he wrote for the duke's entertainment during this time were two *masques: Acis and Galatea* and *Esther.* Masques were similar in structure and format to operas but were designed on a much smaller scale for private performances, using few costumes and uncomplicated sets. Especially noteworthy about these religiously themed pieces is that they were written in English. Handel had written primarily in Italian until this point, dismissing English as a language unsuited to music. Yet these two works are among his greatest, and they were responsible for a major turn in his career as he gradually moved away from Italian opera.

James Brydges, the duke of Chandos. *(Portrait by Herman van der Myn, courtesy of the National Portrait Gallery, London.)*

During his time at Cannons, Handel continued teaching music to the granddaughters of King George I, and he took on at least one other student under the duke's command. It is assumed that he also began teaching music to the son of his copyist John Christopher Smith. These were the only students Handel was willing to endure—he did not have the temperament to deal with poor technique. Out of his teaching experience came a collection of exercises for the harp-sichord. When word got out that the world-famous com-poser had written music exercises, the public came begging for copies. Handel, never missing a chance to turn a profit, published *Suites de Pièces pour le Clavecin (Harpsichord Lessons)* in November 1720.

Handel received sad news while at Cannons: his sister, Dorothea, died on August 8, 1718. Travel was such that he could not possibly have made it from London to Halle in time for the funeral. All he could do was send his sympa-thies, along with some money and gifts. He wrote several times to his brother-in-law that he wanted to visit Halle soon, but he was unable to get away right then. A letter of February 20, 1719 reads:

> Do not judge, I beseech you, my eagerness to see you by the delay in my departure. It is to my great regret that I find myself detained here by unavoidable affairs on which, I venture to say, my fortune depends, and which have stretched out longer than I had believed they would. If you knew the pain that I feel because of not having been able to put into action what I so ardently desire, you would have indulgence for me.

If Handel had left London during this critical time, he might have lost a great opportunity. Efforts had begun at the end of 1718 to put together a new opera company at the Haymarket Theater, one that would require a different kind of management and business plan than had been attempted before. It had become obvious that an opera company could not survive on ticket sales alone, so rather than trying to raise money for each show, this new company would sell shares in the company—the same way investors today buy stock. Shareholders would receive tickets to each season's performances. A board of directors would decide how the money was spent, which operas would be performed, who would write them, and who would star.

Because it was believed that the theater would not succeed without the patronage of the British royals, the new company was called the Royal Academy of Music, and thanks in part to the name, the king himself pledged one thousand pounds per year for five years beginning in May 1719. Fifty-seven more investors were eventually committed: among them seven dukes, thirteen earls, and three viscounts. It took a great deal of time to put this initial list together. The company began soliciting in February 1719 but did not manage to stage an opera until April 1720.

Investors were attracted to the idea of buying shares in the company primarily because the stock market was a relatively new and exciting prospect in England. The South Sea Company, a trading company, had pioneered the idea. For the past year, wealthy Londoners had invested large sums of money. The company attracted investors because it was the only one that traded with islands in the South Seas and South America, where many assumed a great deal of money could be made. As investors kept pumping money into the system, the South Sea Company inflated the value of their stocks from one hundred pounds to one thousand

Giovanni Bononcini (1670-1747) *(Engraving by J. Caldwell.)*

pounds. The concept of getting rich quick was very attractive, and the Royal Academy of Music hurried to get in on the fad.

Handel was one of three composers for the Academy. The other two were the older, more experienced Italians Attilio Ariosti and Giovanni Bononcini. Handel could write operas with uncanny speed, but having two other composers made things go even faster. It is not known if they were paid equally, but one thing is certain—none of them earned nearly as much as the imported Italian singers.

In May 1719, Handel was sent to continental Europe in search of stars. He was given specific instructions not to return without the great *castrato* Francesco Bernardi, better known by his stage name, Senesino. No expense was to be spared in acquiring him, as he was considered by all of London to be the greatest singer in the world.

Castrato singers were men whose testicles had been surgically removed before they reached puberty in order to prevent their voices from changing. The combination of a young boy's vocal cords with the powerful lung capacity of a man produced a unique voice with incredible range.

Castrati were popular throughout the Baroque era, enjoying their greatest fame in Rome (because the pope forbade female singers) and in London (because castrati were considered the ultimate in Italian fashion). Castrati commanded huge fees for their performances and were in constant demand.

Handel found Senesino in Dresden, Germany, with a group of some of the best Italian singers. He and his comrades had been hired to sing in the opera company formed to celebrate the marriage of the crown prince of Saxony, Friedrich August, to Maria Josepha, daughter of Emperor Joseph I of the Hapsburg Empire. Senesino and several other singers agreed to come to England, but they would not be able to arrive until the fall of 1720, which meant the first season of the Royal Academy of Music would have to start without them. The only Italian star Handel managed to secure for the April 1720 opening was Margherita Durastante, the soprano who sang his *Agrippina* in Venice in 1709.

The composer then went to Halle to visit his mother and pay his respects to his recently widowed brother-in-law. Handel's mother was now sixty-eight, and he was her only surviving child.

The great castrato, Senesino. *(Engraving by Charles Grignion.)*

To make up for neglecting his family for so long, especially during their time of mourning, Handel arranged his schedule so that he could spend several weeks with them before returning to London in November.

When the opera season finally opened, King George I and the Prince of Wales were still feuding. But a few insiders knew that a reconciliation between the royal father and son was in the works. Handel's company had access to that inside knowledge, and wisely held off the opening of their first opera. On April 25, the king and his son attended church together for the first time in two years, and that afternoon a political agreement was made to re-appoint Robert Walpole as prime minister of England after a three-year absence. The king had disliked Walpole's politics, but the Prince of Wales made it clear that the Englishman's influence with Parliament was necessary to help make the new royal family more popular. Two nights later, April 27, 1720, the king and the prince attended the opening night of Handel's *Radamisto*. The rest of London clamored for tickets for the opera about Radamisto, a prince, and his wife Zenobia, who must maintain their love in the midst of political intrigue and an attack on their city. The royal reconciliation and the opera were both huge hits.

In August 1720, two months after the close of the first season at the Royal Academy, the South Sea Company went bust. A few savvy investors realized that some of the schemes devised by the company to attract more money were illegal, and they pulled out their money. This precipitated a rush of withdrawals that could not be paid and the company crashed. Hundreds of unsuspecting Londoners lost their fortunes, including the politician Robert Walpole.

The Royal Academy worried that their stockholders would be scared away from investing altogether and would start pulling out, too. They were pleased and surprised to find that most of their subscribers continued to invest in the opera company. It is unlikely that anyone actually thought they would make a profit from theater stocks, but perhaps this investment in the arts seemed harmless compared to the collapse of the South Sea Company.

There was also a great deal of anticipation for the 1720-1721 season because Senesino was scheduled to join the company in September. The composer Bononcini was coming to town as well, ready to introduce his newest opera, *Astarto,* as the first show of the season. *Astarto,* Senesino's London debut, had twenty-four performances, a box-office record Handel was never able to match. Handel spent the summer rearranging *Radamisto* for his new singers and working on a new opera, *Muzio Scevola,* which he composed jointly with Filippo Amadei and Bononcini.

Three composers was two more than an opera usually had, but the board of directors came up with a plan they hoped would attract more ticket buyers—each of the three composers would write one act. The plan worked. Amadei's music, Act I, was light and old-fashioned while Bononcini's Act II and Handel's Act III competed for the most praise. Opera lovers quickly sided with either Bononcini or Handel. It seemed one could not be praised without the other being criticized. The arguments became so ridiculous that the poet

John Byron wrote a satirical verse on the subject.

While the composer challenge piqued interest in the opera for a time, the public was always on the lookout for something new. Handel had a keen eye for what was popular. Senesino drew enormous crowds, and Handel wondered if a female star could duplicate his success. Durastante had left the company to have a baby, so Handel went looking for a new voice. Through connections in Italy, he hired a very popular prima donna named Francesca Cuzzoni. Although she was not attractive, even described as "short and squat, with a doughy cross face" by one observer, Cuzzoni had an exquisite voice. During a performance of Handel's *Ottone,* in December 1722, an audience member stood and shouted, "Damn her! She has got a nest of nightingales in her belly!" Despite the fact that her salary would put a further burden on the Academy, all the directors agreed that Cuzzoni's presence in London would be worthwhile.

Handel's bold move paid off. People were mad for Cuzzoni and Senesino. Houses were packed, and notices had to be put in the papers to keep the outbursts of adoration to a minimum so that the shows could progress in a timely fashion. The poet John Gay wrote in a letter:

> As for the reigning amusement of the town, it is entirely music. . . . There's nobody allowed to say *I sing,* but a eunuch, or an Italian woman. Every body is grown now as a great a judge of music . . . and folks, that could not distinguish one tune from another now daily dispute about the different stiles of Handel, Bononcini and Attilio [Ariosti]. . . . In London and

Westminster, in all polite conversation, Senesino is daily voted to be the greatest man that ever lived.

Working with these talented singers was not always a pleasant experience. Composers and singers were often at odds over who was in charge of the music. Composers saw singers as instruments; singers saw composers as obstacles to their fame and fortune. Cuzzoni once refused to sing an aria Handel had written for her because she was unhappy with the music. Rather than rewrite the piece to suit her taste, Handel threatened to throw his star soprano out the window. In another episode, a tenor told Handel his harpsichord playing was so bad that he (the singer) was going to jump on the instrument. Handel responded, "Let me know when you will do that and I will advertise it: for I am sure more people will come to see you jump than hear you sing."

Of all the singers, Handel had the most trouble with Senesino. The castrato was a huge celebrity and his arrogance was nearly out of control. Durastante, who had come back after her pregnancy, quit the company for good, refusing to work under Senesino's

Francesca Cuzzoni's exquisite voice drew crowds to the Royal Academy productions. *(Engraving by J. Caldwell.)*

shadow. It was impossible to keep everyone happy—tempers flared almost daily.

For the 1722-23 season, Handel wrote *Flavio,* a rare comic opera, and it was hugely popular. The next year, he followed it with his most massive and serious piece yet: *Giulio Cesare in Egitto (Julius Caesar in Egypt),* a drama about Julius Caesar's dealings with Cleopatra. It took him seven months to compose, which for Handel was an unusually long time. With a libretto by Haym and starring six excellent singers, *Giulio Cesare* was Handel's greatest success to date, both artistically and financially. "The house," noted one fan of Handel's work, "was just as full at the seventh performance as at the first."

Title page for a printed edition of Handel's opera *Giulio Cesare. (Courtesy of the British Library, London.)*

Perhaps one of the reasons it took Handel longer than usual to write *Giulio Cesare* was that he had recently purchased a home of his own in London. This house, one of four adjacent dwellings, with its tasteful but simple furnishings, would be his main residence for the rest of his life. No longer would

The house in Lower Brook street (at present, 1839, numbered 57), in which Handel lived and died; — as it appeared before the front of the attic story was raised.

B.aust S. 1839.

Handel's house, No. 25 Brook Street, where he lived from 1723 until his death in 1759. *(Drawing by John Buckler, The British Library, London.)*

he live under the roof of a noble lord. Handel had always looked for independence, and here he finally had it.

Though Handel was doing well, the Academy was still

struggling to make ends meet. For the second year in a row, the stockholders lost money at the end of the season. The solution, the directors decided, was to spend yet more money and hire another Italian star. Faustina Bordoni had all the talent of Cuzzoni plus better looks and a more palatable temperament. Arriving in May 1726, Bordoni quickly captivated the London public. Arguments about whether Bononcini or Handel was the better composer were forgotten amidst heated debates over Cuzzoni's voice versus Bordoni's.

The furor started innocently enough. Handel knew he would never be able to convince one of these singers to take a smaller role than the other in an opera, so he wrote a piece with two lead roles, each with the same number of arias. Audiences came out in droves and were divided over which singer was the best. The show was a huge success, earning eleven performances. It might have run even longer, except that Senesino, for once not the center of attention, claimed to be ill and left London for the warmer climate of Italy.

The tension between the two divas continued to mount through the production of Handel's newest piece, *Admeto,* which opened in January 1727. An observer wrote that the effect of the opera was ruined because the "violence of party for the two singers . . . was so great that when the admirers of one began to applaud, those of the other were sure to hiss." It only got worse when, during a performance of a Bononcini opera on June 6, attended by Princess Caroline of Wales, members of the audience got into an actual brawl—as did the two famous divas themselves. "I humbly propose," one

Faustina Bordoni not only amazed audiences with her voice, she was considered quite beautiful as well. *(Portrait by Bartolomeo Nazuri, Chaucer Fine Arts, London.)*

reporter wrote, "that since these Ladies are not to be reconciled by any other gentle Means, 'tis best that they should fight it out at Figg's or Stoke's Ampitheatre [prize-fighting arenas]; that a subscription be opened for that purpose, and the best woman have the whole house." Handel was outraged by their conduct. He did not take sides, but chastised both equally, calling Bordoni "Beelzebub's spoiled child" and Cuzzoni a "she-devil." The feuding divas stirred up audience interest and helped to sell hundreds of tickets.

On June 11, 1727, word arrived in London that King George I had died in Germany. Just before his death, he had signed the papers granting Handel's request to become a British citizen. Although the king's death was unexpected, it was convenient that Handel, now forty-two, had earned his citizenship just in time to receive his first royal commission from the new king, George II, the forty-three year old son of George I. Handel was to write the coronation music. George II was unhappy with the current court composer, whom he referred to as "that wretched little crooked, ill natured insignificant writer Player and musician." George II went on to announce, "G. F. Hendel should not only have that great honour but . . . choose his own words."

This Handel did, and on a massive scale, composing four of his largest pieces to date, *Zadok the Priest, Let Thy Hand Be Strengthened, My Heart Is Inditing,* and *The King Shall Rejoice.* For the performance on October 11, 1727, Handel engaged forty singers for the choir and an orchestra of one hundred sixty. *Zadok the Priest* has been played at every English coronation ceremony since.

Senesino returned to London when the new opera season began, and Handel wrote three new operas for his stars: *Riccardo Primo, Siroe,* and *Tolomeo. Siroe* was the most popular show of the season, playing nineteen times. But by early 1728, the opera company was despairing because attendance was down. *Tolomeo* only sold enough tickets for seven performances. It seemed as though Italian opera was

William Hogarth's painting depicting a scene from John Gay's satirical *Beggar's Opera,* which played to great success at Lincoln's Inn Fields Theater. *(Courtesy of Tate Gallery, London.)*

going out of style. "I doubt operas will survive the winter," an observer wrote, "they are now at their last gasp. The subscription is expired and nobody will renew it. The directors are always squabbling, and they have so many divisions among themselves that I wonder they have not broke up before; Senesino goes away next winter, and I believe Faustina, so you see harmony is almost out of fashion."

Italian opera was losing favor because Londoners were introduced to something newer and more exciting. In the spring of 1728, Lincoln's Inn Fields Theater opened a production by John Gay called *The Beggar's Opera.* It was a satirical piece written in *pasticcio* style, using parts of songs by many composers. It poked fun at politics, social structure, and, most importantly, Italian opera. This racy entertainment was so popular it ran for ninety performances. None of Handel's Italian operas would be half as successful.

On July 1, 1728, the doors of the Royal Academy of Music closed. The directors had made their final calls on the stockholders, and there was no money left for another season. A month after the final performance the scenery and costumes were auctioned off and the singers returned to Italy. Luckily, this closing didn't devastate anyone financially. In fact, Handel, now forty-three years old, walked away with a tidy sum of money and a good idea of what he would do with it.

Chapter Six
Oratorios

When the Royal Academy of Music closed in July 1728, there were still thirty-five subscribers, including the king, who wanted to continue putting money into the theater. Six months later, a meeting took place among those still willing to support the Academy. An agreement was made for "Hydeger and Hendle to carry on operas without disturbance for five years and to lend them for that time our scenes, machines, clothes, instruments, furniture, etc." In other words, Heidegger and Handel were given permission to reopen the opera house on their own terms—that was, of course, if they could figure out how to get enough money to operate it.

Handel, now forty-four years old, invested nearly all of his savings in the new company, which would be called the New Royal Academy of Music. Records are not clear, but it is likely that Heidegger invested an equal amount. As

George Frideric Handel in a portrait by Balthasar Denner, from about 1728. *(Courtesy of the National Portrait Gallery, London.)*

before, the king put in one thousand pounds per year. The new company still had a board of directors helping to make decisions, but it was no longer funded by shareholders. Instead, patrons could buy a subscription that granted them tickets redeemable for admission to any opera performance throughout the season. This system of funding was innovative for its time, and is similar to the system theater companies use today. It was also much better for Heidegger and Handel, because any profit would go directly into their pockets.

This time around, Handel was the only composer for the theater. Bononcini had taken a steady position working for a patron and Ariosti died unexpectedly before the new season began. Writing an entire season of operas alone was a great deal of work, but Handel lightened his burden by filling out each season with pasticcios and revivals of older works. Again, this was an unusual practice for the era. In Venice, the center of operatic life, operas were rarely revived, if ever. Handel soon discovered that London audiences occasionally enjoyed seeing older works restored with a few modifications.

As soon as the details for reopening the theater were arranged, Handel left England to find a new collection of Italian librettos and singers. Heidegger and the board of governors hoped Handel would convince Senesino to return, but the difficult castrato expected a substantial raise in his salary, and the theater could not afford him. Handel also refused to bring back Cuzzoni, to the despair of the king and others on the governing board. His replacement diva was the less technically polished but more likeable soprano,

Anna Maria Strada. He replaced Senesino with a castrato named Bernarchi.

During his travels, Handel received word from his brother-in-law that his mother had suffered a stroke. He delayed his return to England and spent three weeks (all the time he could spare) with her in Halle. While there, Handel was invited to go to Leipzig to meet Johann Sebastian Bach, but he declined. In Handel's eyes Bach was just a schoolteacher, and the busy composer wanted to spend all the time he had with his dying mother. Handel and Bach never did meet, but Bach composed many influential and beloved works of his own, putting his name on par with Handel's as a master.

Handel returned to London to stage his first opera of the season, *Lotario,* and it was not a hit. One Londoner wrote: "Everyone considers it a very bad opera . . . they are putting on *Giulio Cesare* because the audiences are falling away fast." Most of the complaints were about the singers, who people said did not have the gifts of Senesino or Cuzzoni. One assessment of Strada, the new soprano, was that "her voice is without exception fine, her manner perfection, but her person is *very bad,* and she makes *frightful mouths.*"

Always quick to react to the public's moods, Handel and Heidegger pulled *Lotario* from the boards and readied Handel's new opera, a much lighter piece called *Partenope.* Unfortunately neither *Partenope,* nor the pasticcio Handel assembled to replace it, were very popular. The company stayed afloat due to successful revivals of older operas.

When the season came to an end, Handel released all his singers except Strada. He resigned himself to the fact that

Johann Sebastian Bach (1685-1750) *(Museum für Geschichte der Stadt, Leipzig.)*

Senesino had to be brought back to England, whatever the cost. Senesino's fees were extraordinarily high, and Handel could only hope that the singer would earn his keep.

Handel wrote only one new opera the next year, a light-hearted work called *Poro,* with a libretto by Pietro Metastasio. *Poro* is about an Indian king who is captured by Alexander the Great and must win back his freedom and the woman he loves. For the rest of the season the company performed works chosen to highlight Senesino—both operas he had made famous and operas reconfigured to suit him. Audiences were delighted to have him back, and the theater finally turned a profit.

Handel's joy at the success of the company was tempered

Soprano Anna Maria Strada. *(Courtesy of Albert R. Gellman Collection, Israel Museum, Jerusalem.)*

by the news that his mother had died. He was unable to return home to handle the details of her funeral and estate, and her death signified the end of his ties to his homeland. In order to achieve his dreams, Handel had needed to leave his home and his family, and now they were all gone. For several months, Handel stayed out of the public eye. He was always a private man, but his grief drove him deeper into solitude. During the summer of 1731, Handel was rarely seen out of his house.

Handel's grief affected his work. He had started an opera about the Roman Emperor Titus but could not get past the first act. He gave up on it and began a new work with another libretto by Metastasio. Handel was not working at his usual lightning-quick speed, and did not manage to finish this piece in time for the 1731 season opening. The New Royal Academy of Music had to open with revivals of *Tamerlano, Poro,* and *Admeto.* Handel's new work, *Ezio,* did not open until January 15, 1732. *Ezio,* which tells of a love between a Roman general and the daughter of a wicked man, appealed to King George II—he saw every performance. But the public did not much care for it, and it was shown only five times.

Handel's next work, *Sosarme rè di Castiglia,* which opened a month later, was much more popular and brought in a great deal of money. Handel had shrewdly edited down the *recitatives* (dialogue that serves to advance the plot) because too much Italian bored London audiences. Cutting the dialogue meant the opera made little sense, but only the singers noticed. The plot of the opera involved a king feuding with his son. At the time *Sosarme* opened, King George II and his son, the Prince of Wales, were feuding over power and control in much the same way the current king had with his own father. The similarity between the opera and real-life events was tantalizing to the English public, which loved satire and irony.

Handel's work and the new opera company were thriving, but he had major changes ahead of him, changes that would affect his life and livelihood. It all started when another theater staged Handel's work without his permission.

A benefit concert presented by John Rich, producer of *The Beggar's Opera,* was held on March 31, 1731 at the Lincoln's Inn Fields Theater. Despite the fact that Rich's burlesque musical had played a major role in the first Royal Academy of Music's downfall and that Rich despised the popularity of Italian opera, he had great admiration for Handel's music. Without asking Handel's permission or even letting him know, Rich took *Acis and Galatea,* which

Handel had written in 1721 during his stay at Cannons, and staged it, complete with costumes and scenery. This was the first time the work had ever been performed.

Rich could use Handel's work to his own benefit because copyright laws had yet to be invented. For Lincoln's Inn Fields, Rich adjusted the piece to make it more like an opera, but the work's greatest attraction was that Handel had written it in English. Rich believed English operas could sell tickets, and had seen his theory proved right by the success of *The Beggar's Opera,* which was entirely in English. Now, he repeated that triumph with Handel's own *Acis and Galatea.* All of London rushed to Lincoln's Inn Fields to see it.

The success of this performance did not rile Handel the way we might expect. He had been using the work of other composers for years and could not take offense when someone returned the favor. The only thing that troubled him was that *Acis and Galatea* was drawing audiences away from his opera *Ezio.* Handel was such a good judge of popular sentiment it seems odd he did not realize that his earlier work was a success because it was written in English.

A year later, fellow composer Bernard Gates arranged for a performance of the other masque Handel had composed at Cannons, called *Esther.* The performance would take place on February 23, 1732, in celebration of Handel's forty-seventh birthday. Gates could not turn the work into an opera, as Rich had, because he was using the Chapel Royal choirboys to sing it. The church had approved the choir's participation only under the condition they would not act or wear costumes. So the boys sang *Esther* as an oratorio, an opera minus the fancy dress and staging.

Londoners so desired to see *Esther* that Gates made arrangements with both the London Philharmonic and the Academy of Ancient Music to present it three more times within the next week. These were private performances, and only members of those organizations were allowed to attend.

Princess Anne, daughter of King George II, wanted a production of *Esther* to be presented at His Majesty's Theater so that all Londoners would be able to see and appreciate it, but there were strict rules about where and how the boys' choir could sing. Because the Chapel Royal choirboys were not permitted to perform in a non-religious setting, *Esther* was performed only once more, in a church building. Tickets were sold at five shillings, and this became the first official commercial performance of an English oratorio. This was yet another successful production of

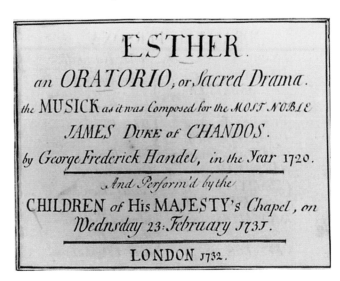

Poster for a London performance of Handel's oratorio *Esther*. *(Courtesy of the Gerald Coke Handel Collection.)*

Handel's own work that he was not involved with.

Handel began to see that there might be a way to profit from oratorios even though they had always been thought of as church music until now. Now he realized that by spicing up an oratorio with new songs and putting stars in the leading roles, he could stage the music at His Majesty's Theater and just might have a new kind of hit on his hands. He spoke to the king about the idea right away.

Soon the *Daily Journal* ran this notice announcing the upcoming production: "By his Majesty's command, at the King's Theatre in the Hay-market, on Tuesday the 2d day of May, will be performed the sacred story of *Esther;* an oratorio in English, formerly composed by Mr. Handel, and now revised by him with several additions, and to be performed by a great number of Voices and Instruments." Handel's Italian stars had to sing in English, some for the very first time. But because they did not have any staging, costumes, or scenery to deal with, there was little to distract them from the music. *Esther* played to six sold-out houses.

Almost overnight, Handel's oratorios became the height of fashion. Thomas Arne, the producer for a new, smaller theater, appropriately called the Little Theater, staged Handel's *Acis and Galatea* on May 17, just as *Esther* was coming to a close across the street. Not to be topped, Handel turned right around and staged his own version of *Acis and Galatea* at His Majesty's Theater in June. The *Daily Journal* reported:

> In the King's Theatre in the Haymarket . . . will be performed a serenata, called *Acis and Galatea,*

formerly composed by Mr. Handel, and now revised by him, with several additions, and to be performed by a great number of the best voices and instruments. There will be no action on the stage, but the scene will represent, in picturesque manner, a rural prospect, with rocks, groves, fountains, and grottoes, amongst which will be disposed a chorus of nymphs and shepherds; the habits and every other decoration, suited to the subject.

Although Handel would not go as far as Arne and call this work a pastoral opera, he did add some scenery and costumes to liven up the production. His new offering was just as successful as *Esther,* with four performances in June and another four in December.

That next summer, Handel received a note from his old friend Aaron Hill who was currently producing an English opera for Arne at the Little Theatre. Hill wanted Handel to write operas in English. "My meaning is," Hill wrote, "that you would be resolute enough, to deliver us from our *Italian Bondage;* and demonstrate, that *English* is soft enough for Opera, when compos'd by poets, who know how to distinguish the *sweetness* of our tongue from the *strength* of it, where the last is less necessary." Handel did have plans for another English oratorio and was tinkering with a few small instrumental pieces, but he simply could not write a full English opera as long as he had a cast of Italian singers. As the summer drew to a close Handel began to concentrate on the upcoming season. He added some Italian arias to *Acis and Galatea* and worked at completing a new Italian opera.

Orlando, about a man who goes mad because he loves a woman he cannot have, premiered on January 27, 1733, and was quite popular even though it was Handel's least conventional composition to date. He tried some unusual techniques, including cutting off arias midway through, and making strange and exciting changes in rhythms and harmonies that had never before been attempted. These alterations focused the opera more on the dramatic unfolding of the plot than on the singing. Though some of Handel's patrons had reservations about the quality of his new music, *Orlando* had an impressive ten-performance run that season and was often revived in the years to come.

Handel's many successful productions may have given him an inflated sense of his own work. He made a grave miscalculation when he produced his next oratorio, *Deborah* (with a libretto by Samuel Humphreys). *Deborah* was written in English, but that novelty was not enough to warrant the prices Handel charged—more than double the ticket prices for Italian operas. To make matters worse, Handel declared that even season ticket holders would have to buy tickets for the performance. (Normally, the money they paid at the beginning of the season granted them admission to the entire season's productions.)

Season ticket holders were so incensed at being asked for more money that at one performance they simply forced their way into the theater without paying. *The Craftsman,* a local paper, published an attack on the composer: "The Absurdity, Extravagancy, and Oppression of *this scheme* disgusted the whole Town. Many of the most constant

Attenders of the *Opera's* resolved absolutely to renounce them, rather than go to them under such Extortion and Vexation."

Around town, Handel was compared to Prime Minister Robert Walpole, who had recently tried to push the Excise Bill through Parliament. This bill would put a heavy tax on liquor and tobacco. There was a barrage of newspaper articles, handbills, and pamphlets—not to mention uprisings—against the proposed bill, and Walpole was forced to withdraw the legislation. He was so unpopular he could not leave his house for fear of being beaten up by London mobs. The same angry rabble that railed against the politics of King George II, who supported Walpole, now targeted Handel. It mattered little that the composer did not take a political stance himself; the simple fact that the king favored him made him a member of the enemy camp.

Deborah opened to an almost empty theater. Handel tried lowering ticket prices, but it was too little too late. Most of aristocratic London had turned against him, and those who would have liked to support the composer were shamed into staying away.

The New Royal Academy of Music was suffering badly by the time the season ended that spring. Ticket sales were down, Handel's reputation had been damaged, and the stress took a toll on his health. He was forty-eight years old, and in crisis. It was time for Handel to reinvent himself. He needed to keep pace with the changing times or be left behind.

Chapter Seven
Competing Troupes

After the disasters of the previous season, Handel needed to do some serious thinking about the future of his opera company. He faced the probability that he would lose what was left of his public support if he did not find a way to adapt his work to the changing tastes of the London public. When the season ended in June 1733, all but one of his Italian singers fled the company. There were serious doubts about whether Handel and Heidegger could pull together a new season for the fall.

Amidst all the turmoil, Handel was invited to have his work performed at Oxford University that summer. This offer must have raised his spirits. He had just finished a new oratorio called *Athaliah,* and now he could premiere it away from London's fed-up audiences, in the bucolic atmosphere of Oxford.

Concerts at Oxford were quite rare—when they occurred, they usually featured the music of the professors or their students. Handel's presence at the school was an honor. Not only was he paid well for his music, the opportunity also gave him a happy few months away from the tension in the capital city.

Unfortunately, after his pleasant summer at Oxford, Handel had to return to London and face the new season. He was out of favor with the London public and his company was bereft of popular Italian singers. And if that was not enough, a new theater company opened across town that featured Italian opera starring the great Senesino—along with most of the rest of Handel's old Italian cast (all but the faithful soprano, Strada). The company was backed by the Prince of Wales and his followers and took the pompous name Opera of the Nobility. They would show performances at Lincoln's Inn Fields Theater, which was managed by the same man, John Rich, who had opposed Handel before.

One newspaper article encouraged Handel to give up, to leave London and go back to Germany, but Handel was not to be deterred. He had a year left of his arrangement with His Majesty's Theater, and he planned to do anything possible to outdo the new company. While he worked hard at his newest opera, his agents were abroad contracting singers. They managed to acquire a castrato named Carestini who had a great deal of fame in continental Europe, and enticed the soprano Durastante back.

Handel opened his season two months before the Opera

of the Nobility did—on October 30, the king's birthday. He revived his opera *Ottone,* starring Durastante. Traditionally, the noble class attended a royal ball on the king's birthday, but in 1733 the entire court came to see Handel's opera instead. Even the Prince of Wales attended, despite his support of the rival company and quarrels with his father. This should have made for a great start to the season, but the second performance had a dismal turnout with no celebrities in attendance. For the rest of the season, Handel staged mostly pasticcios of work by young Italian composers to lure in a new, younger crowd who considered Handel's

Frederick, Prince of Wales, with his sisters. *(Painting by Philip Mercier, National Portrait Gallery, London.)*

own work old-fashioned. It was a good plan, but the box office still suffered.

It had come to be Handel's trademark to save his new work for the second part of the season. This season, it was an opera called *Arianna in Creta (Ariadne in Crete)*. It can hardly have been a coincidence that at the exact same time, the Opera of the Nobility staged *Arianna in Nasso (Ariadne in Nassus)* by Niccolò Porpora, the company's imported Italian composer. The two operas were based on the same Greek myth and were remarkably similar. There is no way to know which company spied on the other first, but the business had always been very competitive. Handel's *Arianna* had a successful initial run of fourteen performances with another six spread out over the spring months. The opening act's minuet was published as a popular piece for violin and harpsichord, and the soprano Strada and Carestini (the castrato) brought the arias to life on stage. One of the most popular of *Arianna's* songs would be sung in English parlors for decades.

Handel still had the complete support of the royal family. Even the Prince of Wales continued to put money into Handel's company, at the urging of his sisters. In March 1734, Princess Anne, the eldest daughter of King George II and one of Handel's music students, married Willem, the prince of Orange. Handel was the only composer given the honor of composing the wedding music.

Despite some success, by the end of the opera season it was clear that Handel's company had failed to compete with the Opera of the Nobility. At the same time, the five-year contract between Handel and Heidegger for use of His Majesty's Theater expired. Heidegger, who remained manager of the theater, threw over his partnership with Handel and rented his theater out to the enemy. Handel knew this meant that the Lincoln's Inn Fields Theater would be empty now, so he went to John Rich to book it for the 1734-35 season. He also knew that Rich was having a brand new space built at Covent Gardens, which would be completed halfway through the season.

Covent Gardens had begun development as London's first town square a century earlier, in 1630. Over time it was filled with churches, shops, and places of entertainment for London's aristocrats. Rich's new, modern theater made Covent Gardens a more popular destination than Lincoln's Inn Fields, the other aristocratic town square of London's West End. Rich suspected that filling his theater with Handel's operas could be profitable, but he insisted upon including dramatic plays in the season as well. Once the deals were done and the papers signed, Handel and his competition had swapped locations.

Whatever hopes Handel and Rich may have had for succeeding at Covent Gardens were quickly dashed. Handel did everything he could think of to please his audiences, struggling to make his productions as different from the Opera of Nobility as possible. He brought in a famous French dancer and added long ballet sequences to his works. He wrote beautiful organ concertos to play during the intervals of his oratorios. Operas had always been staged on Tuesdays and Saturdays, but Handel presented his works on

A view of Covent Garden's piazza and market from the 1700s. *(By Joseph van Aken, The Museum of London.)*

Wednesdays and Fridays. All of these changes helped to give Handel's new opera *Ariodante* eleven performances, but for the most part his work played to sparse crowds and he failed to make a profit.

To make matters worse, Handel's leading castrato, Carestini, quit midway through the season and returned to Italy. The

Opera of the Nobility, on the other hand, was having huge success with a new singer, Farinelli, who was perhaps the most famous and beloved of all the Italian castrati. The Nobility company now had both Farinelli and Senesino, and Handel had nobody.

Without Italian singers, Handel could not stage an Italian opera. He managed to make some arrangements to contract singers after Easter of 1736, but in the meantime, he had no choice but to fill the season with his English oratorios. It was a desperate move that marked another turning point in his career—he created the first oratorio season.

Carlo Broschi, the great Italian castrato known as Farinelli. *(Detail from a painting by Jacopo Amigoni.)*

For the first time in fifteen years, the opera season began without Handel. He waited until February 19, 1736, to unveil his new work, a two-act oratorio titled *Alexander's Feast,* with a libretto by the famous English poet, John Dryden. It featured Strada and a cast of English singers. Handel's calculated move paid off. According to *The London Daily Post:* "Never was upon the like Occasion so numerous and splendid an Audience at any Theatre in London, there being at least 1300 Persons present." He continued the season with revivals of his other oratorios, including *Esther* and *Acis and Galatea,* to more acclaim than he had seen in years.

That spring, London witnessed yet another royal wedding. This time, it was the marriage of Frederick, Prince of Wales, to Princess Augusta of Saxe-Gotha. Handel, hoping to win back the prince's royal patronage, composed an opera specifically to celebrate their union. It was convenient that the royal couple was to be wed at the end of April 1736, for that was exactly the same time that Handel's new Italian singers were finally available to perform. The opera he presented to the royal couple was a romantic piece called *Atalanta,* a story about a king who disguises himself as a shepherd to chase the woman he loves. The final act features a wedding between the two main characters. Prince Frederick and his bride were delighted, and they were also impressed by the choral anthem, *Sing unto God,* that Handel provided for the wedding itself on April 27.

Atalanta, with its beautiful scenery, also impressed the theatergoers of London. It played eight times in May and was revived again the following year by royal command. Perhaps the success of *Atalanta* combined with the renewed support of the prince gave fifty-one-year-old Handel too much confidence—the following autumn, he decided to go back to opera. He composed three new pieces: *Giustino, Arminio,* and *Berenice.* He had a cast of good singers to work with, though none of them had the clout of his old cast, and he intended to make them work hard for their high salaries.

"It is the confined opinion," wrote one of his friends, "that this winter will complete . . . Handel's destruction, as far as loss of money can destroy him." This was the public opinion about all of Italian opera. Even the Opera of the Nobility was suffering. The great stars Senesino and Cuzzoni had left the company, and Farinelli's high voice was no longer such a marvel. Londoners had grown accustomed to what once seemed exotic and no longer flocked to the shows.

Another blow was struck when the church decreed that no operas could be performed on Wednesdays or Fridays during Lent. Handel had to rethink how he normally put a season together and decided that he would do another run of oratorios, including one new work, a re-construction of *Il Trionfo del Temp e Del Disinganno,* which he had written in 1707. Because the oratorios were based on religious themes, the church permitted their performances, and Handel's theater was the only one in town making money during the early spring of 1737.

The Opera of the Nobility went bankrupt and closed its doors on June 11, 1737. This should have delighted Handel in many ways, but he was too sick to take joy in the fact that he had outlasted and outfoxed his competition. The intense work he had done over the last two years had taken its toll. He suffered a stroke on April 13 and in June was still not well. The *Daily Post* reported that "the ingenious Mr. Handel is very much indsipos'd, and it's thought with a Paraletick Disorder, he having at present no Use of his Right Hand, which if he don't regain the Publick will be depriv'd of his fine Compositions." At the age of fifty-two, it looked

A rendering of an oratorio performance.

as though Handel might have reached his end. Even if he recovered from the stroke, a paralyzed right hand meant no composing, no conducting, and no harpsichord playing.

Productions at Covent Gardens carried on while Handel was in his convalescence; his *Berenice* opened on May 18. The public was sympathetic to his illness, but his opera still had weak attendance in spite of this. *Berenice* had the worst run of any Handel opera, playing only four performances before closing.

When the opera season closed, every Italian singer left the country. For the first time since 1729, there were no operas being performed and none were planned for the future. The Opera of the Nobility was bankrupt and Handel was too ill to work. Under the advice of his doctors, or perhaps at the suggestion of his former student the princess of Orange, he decided to go to the steam baths in Germany for treatment. When the word spread that the aging composer was returning to his homeland, it looked as if he was fleeing London; many doubted that he would ever return.

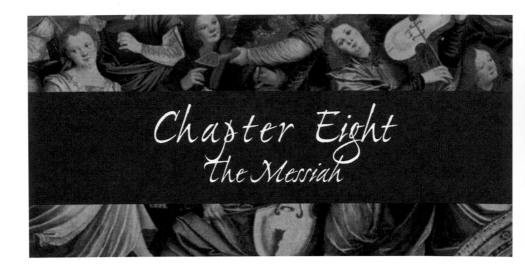

Chapter Eight
the Messiah

Home in Germany, Handel sat in the baths at Aachen, a town famous for its many thermal hot springs. People had been journeying to the town for centuries in hopes of healing their rheumatism, gout, and other ailments. The spring water helped right away—after only one afternoon in the baths, Handel was heard playing the harpsichord in the parlor. Six weeks after he arrived in Germany, he was on his way back to England. It was October 1737, and Handel felt his health had been restored enough to get back to work.

Handel returned to London to find that the theater season had begun without any Italian opera at all. The biggest hit of the season was another anti-Italian opera work from John Rich. Rich had written a kind of sequel to *The Beggar's Opera* called *The Dragon of Wentley,* which had fifty-nine performances that fall. Like its predecessor, *The Dragon of*

Handel in 1737. *(Portrait by G.A. Wolfgang the younger.)*

Wentley was a parody that mocked or satirized many elements of popular culture. The work took several shots at Handel's operas, among other things, though the composer was not upset. Handel took his drubbing in stride, and even commented that he thought "the tunes very well composed." Artists of the time tended to see their work as malleable and important first for its commercial success, for its aesthetic value second. Handel could shrug off mockery because he was still earning a good living in spite of it.

The Dragon of Wentley also took satirical aim at the politics of Robert Walpole, but the Prime Minister was not as good-spirited about it as Handel had been. He retaliated by creating the Licensing Act, a law that required theaters to pay for a permit to produce shows. It also meant Walpole had to approve any play or opera before the public could see it. Handel never had a work turned down, but many other theaters were forced to close their doors. The Licensing Act was extremely unpopular.

Upon his return from Germany, Handel planned to write a new opera—even though he did not have the money or a theater to produce it. He was in the middle of *Farimondo* when the news came that Queen Caroline had died on November 20. Handel had been very close to the queen, having taught music to her daughters for more than twenty years. She had been his champion even when King George II and the Prince of Wales were fighting. He was distraught over her death and wrote a beautiful piece of music titled *The Ways of Zion Do Mourn* for her funeral. All of London was shut down for a six-week mourning period, and Handel abandoned any plans for an opera season that year.

When the theaters reopened, Heidegger, over at the empty Haymarket Theater, was anxious to get the season off the ground. It says something about the fluid nature of the industry that Heidegger approached Handel about a new partnership—even though he had abandoned the composer for his competition only two years before. Handel held no

Queen Caroline *(Mezzotint by John Faber.)*

grudge, but he was no longer interested in producing theater; it was just too much work, and he had too much debt from the last season. He still had not paid some of the singers, and Strada's husband was threatening to sue him and put him in debtor's prison. Needing money, Handel agreed to provide Heidegger with two new pasticcios and two operas *(Farimondo* and *Serse),* for a healthy fee.

Handel's financial situation looked grim. Heidegger and others spent the winter convincing Handel to do a benefit concert for himself. Handel hated the idea of asking for charity, but ultimately he had little choice. Strada's husband insisted on payment, and the composer was nearly bankrupt. He put together a concert of excerpts from his various oratorios and scheduled it for March 28, 1738 at His Majesty's Theater. He hired some exceptional singers and played an organ concerto himself, much to the delight of the more than thirteen hundred audience members. The crowd was so full that five hundred extra chairs had to be put right on the stage. He earned more money in that one night than

Over the years, Handel donated money and music to the Foundling Hospital.

he had for the entire season. He paid Strada and his other pressing debts and began to breathe more easily.

Although people flocked to support Handel for his benefit concert, they still did not rush to see performances of his operas. *Farimondo* only managed eight performances and *Serse* had a mere five. One writer commented that poor ticket sales "reflect[ed] more disgrace on the public than the composer." In the city of London, Italian opera was dead.

Handel's own brush with poverty made him more sympathetic to the plight of others. One afternoon, he saw the children of a recently deceased musician begging for food in the street. He became actively involved with an organization called the Fund for the Support of Decayed Musicians and their Families and for the remainder of his life he gave benefit performances for that group. He also left them a great deal of money in his will.

Another cause that he supported was the hospital for children that housed foundlings and orphans. In eighteenth-century London, unwanted babies were often abandoned, and this hospital provided a home and education for children with nowhere else to go. Handel was unmarried and child-less; his closest relation was a niece he had rarely seen who still lived in Germany. Through Handel's efforts, the hospital had enough money to move and expand from a rented house in Hatton Garden to an estate owned by the earl of Salisbury and, finally, to its own building in 1750.

While Handel was giving some of his attention to helping others, the city of London was making plans to pay tribute to him. On May 1, 1738, a life-size statue of the composer was unveiled at London's Vauxhall Gardens. This was the first time a composer had been so honored while he was still living—Handel was only fifty-three years old. The statue was further unusual because it did not represent him in the stately robes and tall wig he usually wore for portraits. Rather, it shows him wearing informal clothes and holding a lyre in his hands. The statue was meant to represent the pleasure and music that Handel had brought to England.

Charged up with new enthusiasm, Handel returned to the theater for the 1738-39 season. He wrote two oratorios *(Saul and Israel in Egypt)* to librettos by Charles Jennens, a friend who lived in the country outside of London. Handel had often spent summers at his home, and over time Jennens became the principal librettist for Handel's oratorios. Jennens became deeply involved in Handel's composing process, and never hesitated to suggest a change or improvement.

A terracotta model for the statue of Handel, by Louis François Roubiliac. The actual statue was life-size, and displayed at Vauxhall Gardens. (*Courtesy of the Fitzwilliam Museum, Cambridge.*)

Jennens reportedly told Handel his head was "full of Maggots" when Handel moved *Saul'*s important Hallelujah chorus from where it made sense in the story to the final act. Handel must have worked well with Jennens though, and he often made the changes Jennens suggested. He even restored the chorus to its original place—a far cry from his days of threatening to throw sopranos out of windows.

Normally, opera companies gave about fifty performances a season. Between January and May of 1739, Heidegger and Handel only produced fifteen shows—all oratorios. *Saul* impressed those who came to see one of its five performances, but *Israel in Egypt* proved to be a disappointment. *Israel in Egypt* was mainly a choral work, and was missing the operatic solos and arias that audiences loved. It had only one performance. Although some loyal fans wrote to the newspapers begging for a repeat, *Israel in Egypt* was only restaged once the following season, and was not seen again for another sixteen years. Again, people began to whisper that the great composer might be finished.

Based on the limited success of the previous season, Handel had to make a change or he would not be able to continue producing shows. Leaving Heidegger in the lurch, with no company to fill His Majesty's, Handel made arrangements with John Rich to use the smaller theater at Lincoln's Inn Fields for the 1739-40 season. To make his oratorio season more enticing to Londoners, this one would be entirely in English. In the past, many of his oratorios had been arranged with some Italian pieces mixed in, but now he would showcase the language of his audience.

While Handel was focused on shifting from Italian work to English work, a small company at the Little Theater, headed up by Charles Sackville, the earl of Middlesex, was doing the opposite. That group planned to open their season with Italian operettas (light operas) and pasticcios, then move to full operas after the New Year. A small handful of notable Italian singers came to London to participate. Handel was unconcerned about this competition. His instinct for fashion told him Italian opera would not draw the crowds it once had. Besides this, people were more concerned about the war that broke out with Spain in October 1739.

England and Spain had long been enemies, and repeatedly clashed on the high seas. Spain would not involve England in its colonial trade, so the English resorted to smuggling. The Spanish retaliated by conducting brutal ship-to-ship searches. One ship the Spanish singled out was the *Rebecca,* captained by a man named Robert Jenkins. In the clash, Jenkins's ear was cut off by the Spaniards and news of this incident further incensed the English.

The English Parliament and George Walpole, the Prime Minister, were reluctant to go to war against Spain. Robert Jenkins, when called to the House of Commons to testify about the extent of the Spanish cruelty, made a huge stir by brandishing his carefully preserved ear, pickled in brine. When asked what he had done once his ear was cut off, Jenkins replied, famously, that he had given his soul to God and committed himself to his country. Public sentiment was won over, and England declared war—the War of Jenkins's Ear.

The war itself only lasted a few years, and was limited to naval skirmishes in the far-away West Indies, but it made for uneasy times at home, disrupting the economy as people prepared for the worst. In 1739, London was also suffering an extremely cold winter. It was so cold that the Thames river froze. Singers fell ill and shows had to be cancelled. The Lincoln's Inn Fields Theater advertised itself as a safe haven from the cold: the doors would keep out the chill and fires would be blazing inside to keep the hall warm. Despite these efforts, ticket sales suffered at every theater in town.

The year 1740 brought the last operas Handel would ever write: *Imeneo* and *Deidemia.* A collection of Handel's string concertos (Opus 6) premiered and was published later that year, too. These pieces ignored the newer, three-movement concerto style Antonio Vivaldi had recently developed in favor of Corelli's form. Handel's concertos have varying numbers of movements and use a range of tempos and styles, mixing sacred and secular music, lyricism and wit. As Baroque music often does, these concertos contrast many national styles, highlighting typical English, Italian, and German sounds. Many consider Handel's Opus 6 among the finest examples of the concerto form, and the works demonstrate the wealth and range of his inventiveness.

Italian opera seemed to be on the way out, and theater in general was going through hard times. His Majesty's Theater had been empty for two years. The earl of Middlesex and Heidegger tried to convince Handel to throw in with them for the 1741-42 opera season, but he did not see how they could make a success. The composer was at loose ends. Some thought he might return to Germany, but even Handel did not know where he would go or what he would do.

Around this time Jennens sent Handel a libretto for a new oratorio. Handel was intrigued by the text and went to work on the piece at once. The subject of this oratorio was the birth of Jesus Christ, a subject Handel would normally shy away from since religious music was almost always performed only in churches and was generally not profitable. Yet the libretto was strong, and Handel spent from August 22 to September 14, 1741 writing one of the most majestic pieces of music ever heard.

Handel's *Messiah* is vastly different from his other oratorios. There is no obvious drama—no war, no conflict, no love story. Jennens's libretto, which is an arrangement of verses from the Bible, moved the composer to write music that would express the glory and rapture of Christ's birth. Handel drew upon his experience writing opera to build a work that was at once familiar yet strangely new to its audience, one which left them overwhelmed by the beauty and power of its music. The *Messiah* is performed regularly today and many audiences still stand during its Hallelujah Chorus, due in part to the enduring legend that King George II spontaneously rose to his feet the first time he heard it. But after Handel completed the *Messiah,* it would be almost a year before it was performed.

In a surge of creativity after finishing the *Messiah,* Handel moved on to an oratorio called *Samson,* and com-

The final page of Handel's oratorio, *Messiah.*

pleted most of it in just two weeks. His work on *Samson* was interrupted when William Cavendish, the duke of Devonshire and an Irish diplomat, invited him to come to Dublin, Ireland for a season of oratorios. The break from London's struggling and competitive theater scene was exactly what Handel needed. Jennens was very upset at the idea that his *Messiah* would not premiere in England. "I heard with great pleasure at my arrival in Town, that Handel set the Oratorio of *Messiah,*" he wrote to a friend, "but it was some mortification to me to hear that instead of performing it here he was gone into Ireland with it."

To Handel's delight, he found Dublin to be a smaller version of London, complete with an aristocracy that adored the arts. There were several theaters in town, the court employed its own musicians, and the two main churches had large choirs. Some London actors and singers had made their way north over the years to take part in the growing theater community there. Handel's work was going to help establish the newly built Musick Hall on Fishamble Street. Handel was not terribly impressed by the quality of the Irish singers he met, but he made quick work of training them.

Ultimately, Handel assembled a decent cast, pulled mostly from the church choirs, and managed an oratorio season. Tickets for these shows were sold by subscription, with each subscriber getting three tickets per performance. The first six subscription nights, beginning December 23, 1741, were completely sold out. Handel wrote of his delight to Jennens:

> I am emboldened, Sir, by the generous Concern You please to take in relation to my affairs, to give you an

account of the Success I have met here. The Nobility did me the Honour to make amongst themselves a Subscription for 6 nights, which did fill a Room of 600 Persons, so that I needed not sell one single Ticket at the Door. And without Vanity the Performance was received with general Approbation. . . . and the Musick sounds delightfully in this charming Room, which puts me in such spirits (and my Health being so good) that I exert my self on my Organ with more than usual success. . . . I cannot sufficiently express the kind treatment I receive here, but the Politeness of the generous Nation cannot be unknown to You, so I let you judge of the satisfaction I enjoy, passing my time with Honour, profit and pleasure. . . . I shall be obliged to make my stay here longer than I thought.

Handel's music was very well received in Ireland. A comment in the newspaper *Faulkner's Dublin Journal* on December 26 claimed: "The performance was superior to anything of the kind in the kingdom before, and our nobility and gentry, to shew their taste for all kinds of genius, expressed their great satisfaction and have already given all imaginable encouragement to this grand musick."

Before the six performances were finished, Handel was already selling tickets for the next subscription series, which would run through March and April of 1742 and was to include *Alexander's Feast* and a concert version of *Imeneo*. But the real treat for Ireland was still in store—a concert to raise money for charity, featuring Handel's newest and most significant work.

The opening night of *Messiah* was one of the most moving of Handel's career. So many people were anticipated that a leaflet was distributed beforehand requesting that women who planned to attend should leave their hoop skirts at home to make room for more people in the theater. Men were also encouraged to come without swords at their waists, a common part of eighteenth-century formal attire. These requests honored, one hundred extra people squeezed into the Musick Hall.

"On Tuesday last," read an article from the Dublin newspaper, "Mr. Handel's Sacred Grand Oratorio, the *Messiah,* was performed at the New Musick-Hall in Fishamble-street; the best Judges allowed it to be the most finished piece of Musick. Words are wanting to express the exquisite Delight it afforded to the most admiring crowded Audience. The Sublime, the Grand, and the Tender, adapted to the most elevated, majestick, and moving Words, conspired to transport and charm the ravished Heart and Ear."

Chapter Nine
The Last Great Masterpieces

After the success of his *Messiah,* Handel returned to London in September 1742, refreshed and energized but still uncertain of his next move. He wrote to a friend, "Whether I shall do something in the oratorio way (as several of my friends desire) I can not determine as yet."

In the end, Handel decided to try an abbreviated season in 1743, using the subscription pattern that had worked so well in Ireland. He would do two six-performance seasons during Lent, selling subscription tickets ahead of time for box seats and offering gallery tickets at the door. *Samson* was the first production, opening on Ash Wednesday (the first day of Lent), and it successfully ran for all six performances of the subscription. The text for *Samson* was written by Newburgh Hamilton, not Jennens. While Handel respected Jennens's talent, he seemed to prefer working with librettists who, though perhaps less talented were also less difficult.

Because *Samson* was based on an Old Testament story about a Jewish hero who succumbs to the wiles of a seductress but, thanks to his belief in God, overcomes his temptation, the story had particular success with London's Jewish population. Jews did not observe Lent, and there was little in the way of entertainment at that time of year, so *Samson* was particularly welcome. The population of Jewish people in London had grown to about 18,000 between the end of the 1600s and 1743. Many were professionals, and some were members of the middle class. Handel was

savvy enough to recognize the untapped potential of writing for specific audiences, and would design *Joseph and his Brethren* with the Jewish population in mind.

The second six-performance subscription of the Lenten period was filled with three more productions of *Samson,* one of *L'Allegro,* and two of

Kitty Clive was best known as a comic actress. She played the role of Delilah in Handel's *Samson,* and sang in the first London performance of *Messiah.* *(Portrait by Jeremiah Davison c. 1735.)*

Messiah. But the stresses of the past years, his quarrels with Jennens, and the hectic pace of life in the theater had worn down the fifty-eight-year-old composer—he collapsed in May. In the newspapers, his illness was referred to as a "Palsy," which probably means he had another stroke. Amazingly, Handel rested for only a month before returning to work.

That summer, in just under two months, he finished two new oratorios: a secular work called *Semele* and an Old Testament-themed piece called *Joseph and his Brethren*. These works were quite different from each other, with *Semele* structured more like an opera than any of his other oratorios, and *Joseph* being very religious in theme. The librettist, James Miller, was a clergyman who had only written pamphlets and poetry before his efforts with Handel. Any chance of the two working together again ended when Miller died less than a year later.

The oratorio *Semele* tells the story of the Roman god Jupiter's love for Semele, a beautiful mortal, and the goddess Juno's jealousy over the matter. Handel treats the comic story with wit and sensitivity, and blends typical elements of opera (the dramatic love story) with those of oratorio, as the chorus is given a prominent role commenting on the action as the story unfolds. Perhaps because audiences were confused about whether it was an opera or an oratorio, or because the story seemed risqué for Lent, *Semele* was not embraced. It was only in the twentieth century that this piece finally received true appreciation. Like *Samson* before it, *Joseph,* on the other hand, was fairly popular.

Originally, Handel had planned to return to Ireland for another season there, but his tepid success in England stung his pride. He would not leave until he had the city at his feet once more. For the following season, instead of producing just twelve performances over Lent, he would double the amount and begin four months earlier. He planned an ambitious season for 1744-45, including selling fewer subscriptions and more tickets at the door.

Handel wrote a new oratorio for the season called *Hercules.* Neither too secular nor too sacred, it once again blurred the lines between opera and oratorio. The libretto for *Hercules,* by Reverend Thomas Broughton, is about the end of the famous Greek hero's life, focusing mainly on Hercules' jealous wife, Dejanira, who ends up causing his death.

Handel did not forget the popularity of topics such as *Joseph* and *Samson,* and requested a libretto from Jennens about another figure from the Old Testament, Belshazzar. Jennens and Handel were able to reconcile the differences they had in the past, and Jennens agreed to do the work. The story is taken from the biblical book of Daniel and is about Nebuchadnezzar (Belshazzar's father) and a great feast at which writing on the wall prophesized the city's downfall.

Handel was in fine composing form; the music for *Belshazzar* came faster than Jennens could write the words. The work was already in rehearsal before he handed the last act's final draft to Handel, in October 1744.

Unforeseen problems abounded for Handel's early start to the oratorio season. His first production had to be delayed because the date conflicted with a more popular production of Shakespeare's *Richard III*. Some of the cast came down with illnesses that meant performances had to be delayed again. Handel's own health continued to suffer, and was not helped by poor ticket sales. The composer had nearly gone broke trying to entertain the English, and now he sought their sympathy. By mid-January, after only six performances, Handel placed this notice in the newspaper:

> Having for a Series of Years, received the greatest Obligations from the Nobility and Gentry of this Nation, I have always retained a deep Impression of their Goodness. . . . I have the Mortification now to find, that my Labours to please are become ineffectual, when my Expences are considerably greater. To what Cause I must impute the loss of the publick Favour I am ignorant, but the Loss itself I shall always lament.

Handel could not afford to continue the season as planned. He offered to return subscribers' money for the eighteen shows that were now cancelled, but some allowed him to keep it. Bolstered by their belief in him, and by their cash, Handel managed to eke out a few more performances, including three of *Belshazzar*, before closing down. No longer the darling of London, Handel never had another season at His Majesty's Theater.

After the disaster of the previous season, Handel went to the small town of Scarborough in June 1745, in need of peace and rest. He wrote little and did not seem particularly interested in planning a new season at all. His health was poor, his finances were grim, and political affairs made the possibility of a new season doubtful.

In August, England saw an uprising of the Jacobites, a group who contested the legitimacy of George I's inheritance of the English throne back in 1715. The Jacobites were led by Prince Charles, the late Queen Anne's nephew, who they contended was the legitimate heir. The Jacobites and Prince Charles were also Roman Catholic, while the majority of the British population belonged to the Church of England. Catholicism was the religion of France and Spain, two of England's traditional enemies. Because of their common religion, and also in an effort to put a more sympathetic ruler on the English throne, the French offered the Jacobites money and troops. With the promise of French support, Prince Charles gathered an army. In November, Charles and his troops crossed the border from Scotland and began their march on London.

Unfortunately for Prince Charles, a series of mishaps and miscommunications left him without the troops or the resources he expected. George II sent his younger son, the duke of Cumberland, with soldiers to meet Charles and stop him. Charles's forces were weak, poorly armed, and poorly supplied. The duke was able to drive them back to Scotland, where they were eventually defeated.

London's theater plans that autumn were put on hold while the battle raged. Handel, now sixty, offered his support to the English soldiers by writing a patriotic song titled "Song for the Gentlemen Volunteers." Once the Jacobites were defeated, Handel put some thought to a new oratorio, deciding to write something equally patriotic to honor the duke's victory. The king, feeling that it would be inappropriate to celebrate the success of what was essentially a civil war (Scotland was part of the British Empire), did not want a special ceremony, so Handel's *Occasional Oratorio,* as it came to be titled, was the closest thing to a tribute the duke received.

The libretto, by Hamilton, consisted of selections from the Old Testament about the triumph of the righteous. Handel wrote almost no new music for the work, which suggests he may have been ill. While it was not unusual for him to reuse parts of old works, patching a composition together entirely from other sources was. The oratorio was shown three times in February 1746, which amounted to Handel's entire season for that year.

By April 16, 1746, the duke of Cumberland had finally brought the Jacobite revolution to an end. Life in London, particularly where entertainment was concerned, returned to normal. Handel, refreshed, wrote three more new oratorios over the next year, each with a military theme. The success of the *Occasional Oratorio's* patriotic sound, matched by the duke's return to London, no doubt signaled to Handel that martial music could have popular appeal.

With the oratorios *Alexander Balus* and *Joshua,* Handel experimented with more war-themed work drawn from the Old Testament. He wrote these oratorios over the summer of 1746 and filled them with triumphant choruses, military marches, and battle scenes. A third oratorio, *Judas Maccabeus,* features a Jewish hero and tells of the victory of the Jews over the Syrians and is part of the story behind the Jewish holiday Hanukkah. Handel wrote the music in just under a month. It premiered in April and was one of Handel's most successful vocal compositions. Perhaps the combination of military action and religious struggle added to its appeal.

Handel's 1747 Lenten season of oratorios fared much better than those of recent years had. He would continue with the twelve Lent performances for the rest of his career, only changing his policy regarding subscriptions. From now on all tickets were sold at the door, minimizing the risk for investors and encouraging last-minute theatergoers to attend.

Over the summer of 1748, Handel wrote two pieces that would eventually be ranked among his greatest works. He composed *Solomon* and *Susanna* in just three months. Both were a departure from the military themes of the past two seasons, yet were also different from each other. *Solomon* was about the reign of King Solomon at the height of his glory and power. *Susanna* was a light comedy with just enough Biblical context to make it appropriate for Lent.

With *Susanna, Solomon,* and revivals of *Hercules* and *Messiah,* the 1749 oratorio season was far less reverent and serious than others had been since the duke's return from Scotland. Handel had judged his audience correctly: they were tired of war and wanted lightness again. About the premiere of *Susanna,* one noblewoman wrote, "I think I never saw a fuller house."

Messiah's revival brought the work new life and even greater respect. Handel had not staged this oratorio in four years and was thrilled at the enthusiastic reception it received. With the succesful restaging of *Messiah,* Handel was back on top of the theater scene. In fact, *Messiah* has endured as one of the most popular compositions of all time.

In October 1748, the treaty of Aix-la-Chapelle was signed, marking an end to the War of Austrian Succession and the series of conflicts that had included the War of Jenkins's Ear. To celebrate George II's victory and return, Handel was commissioned to write music to accompany a fireworks display to take place on April 27, 1749, at London's Green Park. It was to be an enormous celebration, and Handel rose marvelously to the occasion. His *Music for the Royal Fireworks* is a rich and ornate orchestral piece. An overture in six movements that vary in tempo from adagio to allegro, the piece incorporates fugues and minuets with melodies both serene (as when the subject is the hard-won peace) and jubilant. Handel successfully drew on many of his past masterpieces for this work, and today it is one of his best-loved.

Londoners grew excited as word spread that Handel was composing music for such a grand occasion. Twelve thousand people attended the public rehearsal on April 21, causing a traffic jam on the London Bridge. On the night of the actual performance, almost everyone in the city showed up, paying for entrance to the park or sitting on nearby rooftops. The royal family watched from the Queen's Library. Although the music was superb, and the 101-cannon salute ear-popping, the fireworks turned out to be not only less spectacular than planned, but a disaster. During the display one end of the building housing the fireworks

This painting depicts the grand fireworks celebration on the Thames.

went up in flames, sending people running out of the park.

In May 1749, Handel led a concert of choral and instrumental music to raise funds for the Foundling Hospital. The event brought in a great deal of money. King George II donated two thousand pounds, twice what he had ever given to a season at the opera house. The following year Handel gave the hospital an organ, celebrating the gift with a special performance of *Messiah*. These fundraising concerts would continue for many years, thanks to Handel.

In the summer of 1850, Handel, now sixty-five, took stock of what he owned and realized that he would have something of an estate to leave behind when he died. He wrote his will, leaving large portions of his belongings to his niece, Johanna Friderica, and to Christopher Smith, Senior and Junior, the two men who had stood by him for many years. He left the Foundling Hospital the generous gift of the *Messiah* score, along with the rights to perform it.

Soon after making his will, Handel took a trip to Germany, where he had not been for many years. Most likely, he visited friends and returned to the spa he had enjoyed so many years earlier. Handel was increasingly aware of his mortality as he aged, and he may have wanted to take one last trip to the land of his birth before he died. When he returned to England his health was worse than ever.

In January 1751, Handel began a work, *Jephtha,* which was intended for that year's oratorio season. The piece took him seven months to complete, and would be his final oratorio. Handel continued writing even as he was losing his eyesight to worsening cataracts. Handel noted his age and the date at the end of every line of *Jeptha* and, in the margins, wrote little notes that show his fear that he would be unable to finish the piece in time for the new season.

In the end, Handel was spared from having to admit that he had no new music because all forms of entertainment in England were brought to an abrupt close when the Prince of Wales died in March. The English public never knew that Handel's new oratorio was incomplete, and he was able to hide his declining health.

By the summer of 1751, Handel had completely lost the use of his left eye, and his right eye was beginning to fail. The sections of *Jephtha* written during this period are full of erasures and blots, rare marks for a Handel score. Losing his eyesight was a torment, and, desperate to be healed, he underwent surgery to have his cataracts removed in November 1852. The surgery was extremely primitive and was performed without anesthesia. The doctor used a needle to pierce the cornea of each eye and push the cataracts below the pupils. Handel's eyesight was temporarily improved by this surgery, but by January 1753 (two months later) he was completely blind.

Except for a short trip to Bath, Handel spent the rest of 1752 quietly in his home. The younger Christopher Smith was with him most of time. Smith had become an accomplished musician under Handel's tutelage and helped with his writing and copying. Over the next oratorio season he even stepped in to play for the composer on the harpsichord. Only a few close friends knew how precarious Handel's health was at this time, and they took pains to tell their acquaintances not to miss the oratorio season because there probably would not be another. Their dire warnings proved unfounded; with the help of Smith Junior and a blind organist named John Stanley, Handel continued to produce oratorio seasons for another six years, until within a week of his death.

When Handel's blindness was finally revealed to the public, it was seen as a great tragedy. One of his greatest supporters in London, Lady Shaftesbury, wrote, "I went last Friday to 'Alexander's Feast'; but it was such a melancholy pleasure, as drew tears of sorrow to see the great though unhappy Handel, dejected, wan, and dark, sitting by, not playing on the harpsichord, and to think how his light had been spent by being overplied in music's cause." Handel's blindness did put an end to his composing, but he did not stop playing the harpsichord altogether. Full of pride and

Handel in 1756, with the *Messiah* score visible on the desk to his right. Painted by Thomas Hudson, this is the only known portrait of the composer once he became totally blind. *(Courtesy of the National Portrait Gallery, London.)*

determination, he played concertos in between the acts of the oratorios, allowing Smith Junior or Stanley to lead the oratorios themselves. He played from memory, as exquisitely as ever and with the same passion and precision that had made his reputation as a young man.

Handel kept to himself more and more as the years passed, coming out only for his concerts and fundraisers for the hospital. In August 1758, Handel made one more futile attempt to restore his sight. A quack surgeon named John Taylor arrived in London promising a cure. Coincidentally, Johann Sebastian Bach had also suffered from cataracts, and Taylor had operated on his eyes, too. Bach's operation was a total failure, and may have actually hastened his death, but Handel had no way to know this. Handel's surgery went somewhat better than Bach's—it did not cause any further complications, but it did not cure his blindness, either.

Over the next year Handel's health waned further. His appetite, which had always been abundant, decreased to the point that he was barely eating at all. The portly old man became weaker and weaker as the months passed. On April 6, 1759, Handel performed for the last time, playing harpsichord for a staging of *Messiah* at Covent Gardens. It had been his plan to set out for Bath soon after to take another water cure, but as he exited the theater that night he collapsed.

Rushed home by carriage, Handel spent the following week in and out of a coma. One afternoon he was alert enough to make a few final changes to his will, mostly to give money to more charities and friends who had become important to him in his last days. Handel bequeathed the generous gift of a year's salary to his house servants.

Fate had it that the man who had toiled his hardest every year at Easter time was dying during the week of Easter. He died in his sleep, between midnight and dawn, on Saturday April 14, 1759.

In his will, Handel had requested a private funeral, but it was hardly an intimate affair. A massive choir was formed

A terracotta model for the Handel monument at Westminster Abbey. *(Courtesy of The Ashmolean Museum, Oxford.)*

from the three largest churches in London and more than 3,000 people attended his burial in the South Cross at Westminster Abbey. The *Whitehall Evening Post* announced, "A monument is to be erected for him, which there is no doubt but that his Works will even outlive." Handel's stock had risen and fallen many times over the years, and his famous temper was not soon forgotten. But his death reminded the country how much it had loved his music, and for that, everything was forgiven.

While he was alive, Handel was most famous for his Italian operas. Today, although his operas are still performed regularly at major houses, they are the least popular of his works. Handel's concertos and oratorios have been his enduring legacy. They are studied and performed daily in music schools, concert halls, and churches worldwide. *The Water Music* and his *Music for Royal Fireworks* have been used in film, television, advertising, and educational toys. Of all his works, *Messiah* remains the most well known and loved. It is performed in thousands of venues every Christmas—from amateur sing-a-longs at community theaters to five-thousand-seat concert halls—all over the world. Handel's works have proven to be the lasting monument to his memory.

Timeline

1685   On February 23, George Frideric Handel is born in Halle, Germany.

1692   Handel plays organ at the court of Weissenfels.

1693   Begins music lessons with Wilhelm Zachow.

1697   Handel's father dies on February 11.

1702   Enrolls at Halle University and meets G.P. Telemann.

1703   Earns post as violinist in Gänsemarkt Orchestra; in July, meets musician/music critic Johann Mattheson in Hamburg, the two become immediate friends.

1704   Handel assists Reinhard Keiser in composing *Easter Passion;* Handel composes his first opera, *Almira.*

1705   Composes second opera, *Nero.*

1707   Handel goes to Italy; in Rome, writes his first oratorio; in Florence, stages his first Italian opera, *Rodrigo.*

1709   Stages *Agrippina* in Venice.

1710   Becomes kapellmeister to Elector George Ludwig in Germany.

1711   Premieres *Rinaldo* in London.

1712   Composes *Il Pastor Fido.*

1713   In January, Handel premieres *Teseo.*

1714   Queen Anne of England dies on August 1; Elector George of Hanover inherits the throne, becoming king.

1717   Handel composes *Water Music* for a special celebration hosted by King George I.

1718   Handel's sister, Dorothea, dies on August 8.

1720   Royal Music Academy opens with first opera; in August, South Sea Company folds; second season for Royal Music Academy begins with Italian stars Senesino and Cuzzoni.

1722   Third season at Royal Music Academy features Handel's *Flavio* and *Giulio Cesare.*

1726   In May, Italian diva Faustina Bordoni joins the Royal Music Academy.

1727   On June 11, King George I dies; George II takes the throne.

1728   *Beggar's Opera* opens at Lincoln's Inn Fields; on July 1, Royal Academy of Music goes out of business.

1729   In December, Handel reopens the opera company with *Lotario.*

1730   Handel's mother dies.

1731   John Rich stages Handel's oratorio *Acis and Galatea.*

1732   Handel stages *Esther,* an English oratorio.

1733   Handel composes the opera *Orlando* and the oratorio *Deborah.*

1735   Handel moves his opera company to Covent Gardens.

1736   Premieres *Alexander's Feast.*

1737   Handel has a stroke on April 13.

1739   Composes *Saul* and *Israel in Egypt.*

1741   Composes *Messiah* and it premieres in Ireland.

1746   Composes *Occasional Oratorio* for duke of Cumberland.

1749   Handel's *Fireworks Music* is played at a huge outdoor celebration on April 29.

1751   Handel composes *Jephtha,* his final oratorio.

1758   Handel undergoes eye surgery.

1759   On April 14, Handel dies in his London home; buried at Westminster Abbey on April 20.

Glossary of Musical Terms

anthem An instrumental work for a celebration or important event.

aria A solo in an opera used to demonstrate both the emotion of the character and the vocal abilities of the singer.

ballet A classical form of dance, incorporating movement, music, and scenery to convey a story, theme, or atmosphere.

Baroque era A period in history that dates roughly from 1600 to 1750. The most famous composers from this era are Bach, Vivaldi, and Handel.

benefit performance A concert in which all the money from ticket sales goes to a charitable cause.

cantata A religious play without scenery or staging that is sung by a choir, usually with soloists and an orchestra.

castrato A male singer whose pre-pubescent high voice is retained through castration.

clavichord A small keyboard instrument popular in the Renaissance, differing from others of the time because its strings were struck (like pianos) rather than plucked (like harpsichords).

choir A vocal ensemble whose singers sing in parts, with a number of voices singing each part.

choral Belonging to the choir; also full, or for many voices.

composer One who writes music.

concerto A piece of instrumental music which highlights a particular instrument.

countertenor The highest male voice in an opera, displaying an unusually high range (similar to a female alto or soprano), often achieved through falsetto.

debut A singer or musician's first performance.

dedication When a composition is offered in tribute to a particular person or cause.

diva Literally, "divine." A term used to describe female opera singers.

duet A piece for two musicians.

ensemble A collection of musicians who play together as a group.

falsetto The technique by which mature male voices can reach the high notes of the (female) alto or soprano, which are usually outside the range of the male vocal cords.

harpsichord A keyboard instrument whose strings are plucked by quills. Most popular in the Renaissance and Baroque eras, it predated the piano (whose strings are struck).

impresario Much like a producer, this is the person who raises the money for a theatrical production.

Jubilate A musical setting of the 100th Psalm in the St. James Bible.

kappelmeister The conductor of a court theater.

librettist One who writes the words and story of an opera.

libretto The text of an opera.

masque A small-scale opera, with few costumes and simple sets.

minuet A musical piece in slow three-quarter time. A popular dance, the form originated in France.

oboe A double-reed woodwind instrument.

ode A poem or musical work that honors a particular person, event, or object.

opera Originating in seventeenth-century Italy, a story set to music, usually entirely sung. Music, drama, scenery, costumes, dance, and other theatrical elements combine to make the art form complete.

operetta A lighter form of opera, featuring spoken dialogue along with songs and dances. Comparable to a Broadway musical of today.

opus Literally, "work."

oratorio Usually Biblical stories set to music. As with opera, these stories are sung, but (unlike opera) oratorios do not make use of elaborate staging.

orchestra A group of instrumentalists divided into wind, brass, percussion, and string sections.

organ A large keyboard instrument, made of tall pipes through which air passes to produce sound.

Passion A grand cantata about the life and death of Jesus Christ (usually performed at Easter).

pasticcio Literally, "pasty." Passages taken from numerous other sources by various composers are pasted together to make a new composition.

patron One who financially supports an artist's work.

postlude A composition, often for organ, to be played at the end of a church service as the parishioners leave. Also, a piece of music that concludes a larger composition.

prima donna The female star of an opera.

premiere The first performance of an opera or musical work.

prelude A composition for the organ to be played as parishioners enter a church. Also, the opening piece of music that introduces a larger compositon.

prodigy A child with exceptional musical ability.

publication A music manuscript that has been set in print and is sold for profit.

recitative The conversational, narrative songs used to further the plot of an opera.

repertoire The list of pieces that a given performer or ensemble is prepared to perform.

revival A performance of an opera from a past season.

royalties The fees collected by the artist for the sale and performance of his work.

score The instrumental and vocal parts of a composition as written out in musical notation.

season The stretch of time each year during which theatrical and operatic shows are performed, usually from October through June.

sacred From or having to do with the church.

secular Not religious.

serenata A dramatic cantata; instrumental music combining elements of chamber and symphonic music and generally played outdoors in the evenings or at social events.

soprano The leading female singer in an opera or the highest voice in a choir.

subscribers Those who support a theater or theatrical company by purchasing a season's worth of tickets.

Te Deum Literally, "to God." A hymn of praise.

tenor The highest natural male voice in a choir.

violin A four-stringed musical instrument played with a bow.

virtuoso An expert performer on a particular instrument.

Sources

CHAPTER ONE: A Precocious Child

p. 16, "Ah! bitter grief! my dearest father's heart..." Donald Burrows, *Master Musicians: Handel* (Oxford: Oxford University Press, 1994), 9.

CHAPTER TWO: Hamburg

p. 22, "We played on almost all the organs..." Christopher Hogwood, *Handel* (New York: Thames and Hudson, 1984), 23.

p. 24, "At that time he composed very long, long..." Ibid., 23.

p. 28, "No harm came of the affair..." Ibid., 24.

CHAPTER THREE: Italian Sojourn

p. 33, "to the amazement of everybody" Herbert Weinstock, *Handel* (New York: Alfred A. Knopf, 1946), 29.

p. 37, "is a good looking man and talk is..." Hogwood, *Handel,* 39.

CHAPTER FOUR: Her Majesty's Theater

p. 46, "Mr. Handel the Orpheus of our century..." Hogwood, *Handel,* 62.

p. 47, "Tuesday, the 6th of February, being the Queen's Birthday..." Burrows, *Master Musicians,* 66.

p. 49, "The Scene represented only the Country..." Ibid., 70.

p. 50, "He [Boyle] possessed every quality of a genius..." Hogwood, *Handel,* 68.

p. 52, "The day that gave great Anna birth…" Weinstock, *Handel,* 67.

p. 55, "Whereas by the frequent calling for…" Ibid., 74.

p. 57, "His majesty approved of it so greatly…" Hogwood, *Handel,* 72.

CHAPTER FIVE: The Royal Academy

p. 62, "Do not judge, I beseech you…" Weinstock, *Handel,* 91.

p. 68, "short and squat, with a doughy cross face" Hogwood, *Handel,* 83.

p. 68, "Damn her! She has got a nest…" Ibid., 83.

p. 68, "As for the reigning…" Weinstock, *Handel,* 115.

p. 69, "Let me know when you will do that and I will…" Burrows, *Master Musicians,* 115.

p. 70, "The house was just as full…" Hogwood, *Handel,* 84.

p. 72, "violence of party for the two singers…" Ibid., 86.

p. 72, "I humbly propose that since…" Weinstock, *Handel,* 133.

p. 73, "Beelzebub's spoiled child…she-devil." Ibid., 133.

p. 74, "that wretched little crooked, ill natured insignificant writer…" Burrows, *Master Musicians,* 123.

p. 75, "I doubt operas will survive the winter" Hogwood, *Handel,* 88.

CHAPTER SIX: Oratorios

p. 77, "Hydeger and Hendle to carry on operas…" Burrows, *Master Musicians,* 127.

p. 80, "Everyone considers it a very bad opera…" Hogwood, *Handel,* 93.

p. 80, "her voice is without exception fine…" Ibid., 92.

p. 86, "By his Majesty's command…" Weinstock, *Handel,* 163.

p. 86, "In the King's Theatre in the Haymarket…" Ibid., 165-6.

p. 87, "My meaning is that you would be resolute enough…" Burrows, *Master Musicians,* 172.

p. 88, "The Absurdity, Extravagancy, and Oppression of *this scheme...*" Hogwood, *Handel,* 105.

CHAPTER SEVEN: Competing Troupes

p. 96, "Never was upon the like Occasion so numerous and splendid..." Burrows, *Master Musicians,* 188.

p. 98, "It is the confined opinion..." Hogwood, *Handel,* 135.

p. 98, "the ingenious Mr. Handel is very much..." Ibid., 137.

CHAPTER EIGHT: The *Messiah*

p. 101, "the tunes very well composed." Hogwood, *Handel,* 144.

p. 104, "reflect[ed] more disgrace on the public than the composer." Ibid., 147.

p. 106, "full of Maggots" Burrows, *Master Musicians,* 202.

p. 111, "I heard with great pleasure..." Burrows, *Master Musicians,* 260.

p. 111, "I am emboldened, Sir, by the generous Concern..." Weinstock, *Handel,* 235-6.

p. 112, "The performance was superior..." Ibid., 237.

p. 113, "On Tuesday last Mr. Handel's Sacred Grand Oratorio..." Hogwood, *Handel,* 175-76.

CHAPTER NINE: The Last Great Masterpieces

p. 114, "Whether I shall do something in the oratorio way..." Burrows, *Master Musicians,* 267.

p. 118, "Having for a Series of Years, received the greatest Obligations..." Burrows, *Master Musicians,* 281.

p. 121, "I think I never saw a fuller house." Hogwood, *Handel,* 213.

p. 125, "I went last Friday to 'Alexander's Feast'..." Hogwood, *Handel,* 225.

p. 128, "A monument is to be erected for him..." Weinstock, *Handel,* 305.

Bibliography

Bettmann, Otto L. *Johann Sebastian Bach As His World Knew Him.* New York: Birch Lane Press, 1995.

Burkofzer, Manfred F. *Music in the Baroque Era.* New York: W.W. Norton & Company, Inc., 1947.

Burrows, Donald. *Master Musicians: Handel.* Oxford, UK: Oxford University Press, 1994.

Carlin, Richard. *European Classical Music 1600-1825.* New York and Oxford: Facts on File Publishing, 1988.

Carswell, John. *From Revolution to Revolution: England 1688-1776.* New York: Charles Scribner's Sons, 1973.

Catucci, Stefano. *Masters of Music: Bach and Baroque Music.* New York: Barron's Educational Series, Inc., 1997.

Clifford, James L., ed. *Man versus Society in Eighteenth-Century Britain: Six Points of View.* New York: W. W. Norton & Company Inc., 1968.

Fulbrook, Mary. *A Concise History of Germany.* Cambridge, UK: Cambridge University Press, 1990.

Hibbert, Christopher. *London: The Biography of a City.* New York: William Morrow & Company, Inc., 1969.

Hill, Brian W. *Sir Robert Walpole.* London: Hamish Hamilton, 1989.

Hogwood, Christopher. *Handel.* New York: Thames and Hudson, 1984.

Inwood, Stephen. *A History of London.* New York: Carroll &
Graf Publishers, Inc., 1998.

Quennell, C. H. B. & Marjorie. *A History of Everyday Things
in England,* Vols. II and III. New York: G. P. Putnam's Sons,
1961.

Russell, Francis. *The Horizon Concise History of Germany.*
New York: American Heritage Publishing Co., Inc., 1973.

Sadie, Stanley. *The New Grove Dictionary of Music and Musicians.* Washington, D.C.: Macmillan Publishers Limited,
1980.

Weinstock, Herbert. *Handel.* New York: Alfred A. Knopf, 1946.

Web sites

Baroque Composers and Musicians
www.baroquemusic.org

George Frideric Handel site
www.gfhandel.org

Handel House Museum
http://www.handelhouse.org

Humanities Web
http://www.humanitiesweb.org
Terrific resource for music history with comprehensive information on composers and periods ranging from medieval times
to the present.

The Internet Public Library's Music History 102
www.ipl.org/div/mushist
A guide to Western composers and their music from the Middle
Ages to the present.

Wonderful World of Music History
www.chsdragonband.com
Offers a general overview of periods in music history, bio-
graphical information on composers, and links to other helpful
sites. Maintained by high-school music students.

Index

Amadei, Filippo, 67
Anne, Princess, 85, *92,* 93, 99
Anne, Queen of England, 41, 46-
    47, *48,* 52-54, 119
Ariosti, Attilo, 64, 69, 79
Arne, Thomas, 86-87
Augusta, Princess of Saxe-Gotha,
    97

Bach, Johann Sebastian, 22, 42,
    56, 80, *81,* 127
Bernarchi, 80
Bernardi, Francesco (Senesino),
    64-65, *65,* 67-70, 72, 74-75,
    79-81, 91, 96, 98
Bononcini, Giovanni, 45, 64, *64,*
    67, 69, 72, 79
Bordoni, Faustina, 72-73, *73,* 75
Boyle, Richard, 50-52, *51*
Broschi, Carlo (Farinelli), 96, *96,*
    99
Broughton, Thomas, 117
Brydges, James, duke of
    Chandos, 59, 61
Buxtehude, Dietrich, 22-23, *23*

Carestini, 91, 93, 95
Caroline, Princess of Wales, 48,
    54-55, 72, *92*
Caroline, Queen, 102, *103*
Cavendish, William, 111
Charles, Prince, 119
Clive, Kitty, *115*

Corelli, Arcangelo, 33, 35, *35,*
    109
Covent Gardens, 94, *95,* 99, 127
Craftsman, The, 88-89
Cuzzoni, Francesca, 68-69, *69,*
    72-74, 79-80, 99

Daily Journal, 86
Dryden, John, 96
Durastante, Margherita, 65, 68-
    69, 91-92

Ernst August, duke of Hanover,
    40-42

Faulkner's Dublin Journal, 112
Feustking, Friedrich Christian, 27
Foundling Hospital, 104-105,
    104, 123
Frederick, Prince of Wales, 83,
    91-93, *92,* 97, 102, 124
Friedrich August II, Elector of
    Saxony, 65
Fund for the Support of Decayed
    Musicians, 104

Gänsemarkt Opera House, 22, 24,
    26, 29
Gates, Bernard, 84-85
Gay, John, 68, 74
Geminiani, Francesco, 54
George I, Elector of Hanover and
    King of England, 40-41, *41,*

48, 53-59, 61, 63, 66, 74
George II, King of England, 58-59, 66, 74, 83, 89, 93, 102, 110, 119, 122-123
Grimani, Cardinal Vincenzo, 38, 40

Hamilton, Newburgh, 114, 120
Handel, Dorothea (mother), 15-17, 55, 65-66, 80, 81-82
Handel, Dorothea (sister), 62
Handel, George (father), 11-16, *13*, 85
Handel, George Frideric, *10, 16, 28, 78, 101, 106, 126, 128*
  Appetite, 51, *53*
  Birth, 14
  Compositions
    Acis and Galatea, 60, 83-84, 86-87, 97
    Admeto, 72, 82
    Agrippina, 38, 40, 65
    Alexander's Feast, 96, 112, 125
    Almira, 27, 29-30, *30,* 36
    Belshazzar, 117-118
    Berenice, 97, 99
    Deborah, 88-89
    Esther, 60, 84-87, *85,* 97
    Ezio, 82, 84
    Farimondo, 102-104
    Giulio Cesare in Egitto, 70, *70,* 80
    Hercules, 117, 121
    Il Pastor Fido, 48-49
    Imeneo, 108, 112
    Israel in Egypt, 105-107
    Jephtha, 124
    Joseph and his Brethren, 115-117
    Messiah, 109-113, *110,* 114-116, 121-123, *126,* 127, 129
    Music for Royal Fireworks, 122, *123,* 129
    Ottone, 68, 92
    Radamisto, 66-67
    Rinaldo, 46-49, *46*
    Rodrigo, 36-37, 40
    Samson, 110-111, 114-117
    Saul, 105-106
    Teseo, 49-50, 55
    Triumph of Time and Truth, The, 34-35, 98
    Water Music, 56, 57-58, *57,* 129
    Ways of Zion Do Mourn, The, 102
  Death, 128
  Early compositions, 24-25
  Father's death, 16
  Illness, 98-99, 119, 124-125, 127-128
  Mother's death, 81-82
  Musical education, 13-16
  Other compositions, 30, 31, 52, 53, 56, 62, 67, 70, 74, 80, 82, 88, 90, 95, 97, 108, 115, 119, 120
  Plagiarism, 36-37, 46, 48
  University studies, 17-18, 20
Handel, Karl, 11
Haym, Nicola Francesco, 49, 55, 70
Her Majesty's Theater, 46, 48, 50
Heidegger, Johann Jacob, 50, *50,* 55, 77, 79-80, 90, 94, 102-103, 106-107, 109
Hill, Aaron, 45-46, 48-49, 87
His Majesty's Theater, 55, 58, 86, 91, 94, 103, 107, 109, 118
Humphreys, Samuel, 88

Jacobites, 119
Jenkins, Robert, 108

Jennens, Charles, 105-106, 109-111, 114, 117
Johann Adolf, duke of Weissenfels, 11-13
Johann Adolf VI, Duke, *56*
Joseph I, Holy Roman Emperor, 65

Keiser, Richard, 26-27

Lincoln's Inn Fields Theater, 74, *74,* 83, 91, 94, 107-108
Little Theater, 86-87, 107
London Daily Post, 96, 98

MacSwiney, Owen, 49-50
Maria Josepha, 65
Mattheson, Johann, 22-24, *24,* 27-29
Medici, Ferdinand de', 40
Medici, Gian Gastone de', 31
Metastasio, Pietro, 81-82
Miller, James, 116
Monteverdi, Claudio, 25, *25*

New Royal Academy of Music, 82, 89

Opera Register, 49
Opera of the Nobility, 91-94, 96, 98-99
Ottoboni, Cardinal, 33-35, *34*

Pamphili, Cardinal, 34-35
Porpora, Niccolò, 93

Reinken, J. Adam, 21-22, *23*
Rich, John, 83-84, 91, 94, 100, 107
Rossi, Giacomo, 46, 48
Royal Academy of Music, 63-67, 71, 76, 77, 83
Ruspoli, Marchese Francesco, 35-36, 38

Sackville, Charles, 107, 109
San Giovanni Church, 33
San Giovanni Grisostomo Theater, *39*
Scarlatti, Alessandro, 33, 45
Scarlatti, Domenico, 33, *36,* 40
Shakespeare, William, 44, 118
Smith, John Christopher, 55-56, 61, 123
Smith, John Christopher, Jr., 55-56, 61, 123, 125, 127
Sophia, Electress of Hanover, 37
South Sea Company, 63, 66-67
St. Marion's Church, 22
Stanley, John, 125, 127
Strada, Anna Maria, 80, *82,* 91, 93, 103-104

Tarquini, Victoria, 37
Taust, Anna, 15-16
Taylor, John, 127
Teatro Civico Accademico, 36
Telemann, George Phillip, 17-18, *18,* 29, 56
Thiele, Johann, *23*
Thirty Years War, 19-20, 21, 26

Utrecht, Peace of, 52-53

Vivaldi, Antonio, 40, 109

Walpole, Robert, 66-67, 89, 102, 108
Walsh, John, 47
War of Austrian Succession, 122
War of Jenkins's Ear, 107-108, 122
Westminster Abbey, 128
Whitehall Evening Post, 128
Willem, Prince of Orange, 93

Zachow, Wilhelm, 14, 16